SOUL
FEATHERS

An anthology to aid the work of
MACMILLAN CANCER SUPPORT

Indigo Dreams Publishing Ltd

First Edition: Soul Feathers
First published in Great Britain in 2011 by:
Indigo Dreams Publishing Ltd
132 Hinckley Road
Stoney Stanton
Leics
LE9 4LN
www.indigodreams.co.uk

ISBN 978-1-907401-36-7

British Library Cataloguing in Publication Data. A CIP record for this book can be obtained from the British Library.

Designed and typeset in Galliard BT and Garamond by Indigo Dreams

Cover design by Ronnie Goodyer at Indigo Dreams.

Printed and bound in Great Britain by Imprint Academic, Exeter.

Papers used by Indigo Dreams are recyclable products made from wood grown in sustainable forests following the guidance of the Forest Stewardship Council.

Dedication

To my brave Dad, Ian,
who continues along life's footpath
and my beloved Granddad, Jack
who walks with angels

Anne Deborah Morgan
Co- Editor 'Soul Feathers'

His Royal Highness has asked me to wish you every success with the book 'Soul Feathers'.
Mark Leishman, Private Secretary to TRH The Prince of Wales

The Prime Minister greatly appreciates the excellent work of Macmillan Cancer Support and hopes that the anthology is a great success.
Matthew Style, Private Secretary to Rt Hon David Cameron, MP

I wish you every success with Soul Feathers and fundraising. My comment on Hope would be "Never give up on hope, it can be your 12th man right up until the 93rd minute!"

Sir Alex Ferguson CBE, Manager, Manchester United F.C.

I know only too well the effects of cancer having lost my own mum to lung cancer. I am delighted to give my support to Indigo Dreams Publishing and all connected with 'Soul Feathers'. I hope it exceeds all expectations for Macmillan Cancer Support.
Gaby Roslin.

Acknowledgements

I would like to thank everybody who has contributed to the anthology and those whose poetry could not be included.

My special thanks go to Ronnie Goodyer and Indigo Dreams for making the vision a reality, Sue Tiplady for her faith in me and for choosing the anthology's theme and Chrys Salt, my 'unofficial mentor', for her support and guidance. I would also like to give a special thank you to Andrea Wren for plugging the project on her blog and to Tom Leonard and Richard Berengarten for spreading the word.

I would also like to acknowledge Michael Chapman-Johns who was one of the first people to join my Facebook group and publicise the project. Shortly afterwards, his brave fiancé, David Johns, sadly lost his battle with cancer.

Finally, I would like to thank my Mum and Dad, Denise, Hatty and Rachel for their continued love and support.

A note from Indigo Dreams

All authors who have their work included and those who have granted permission for work to be included in this anthology have donated their time, energy and talent for the benefit of Macmillan Cancer Support.

We at Indigo Dreams Publishing Ltd would like to applaud and thank each of them.

A few words from Annie....

Firstly, I would like to thank you for purchasing this anthology, which I know you will enjoy reading.

The idea of publishing a poetry anthology to raise money for Macmillan Cancer Support came to me about a year ago. I chose Macmillan because it is a charity close to my heart. I have always admired the work of the Macmillan nurses and like so many people who have contributed to this anthology I have watched loved ones battle with cancer. I arranged a meeting with Sue Tiplady, then of Macmillan, and over a latté or two, I shared my vision for the anthology. Sue suggested the general theme of 'hope' which I embraced wholeheartedly.

What I needed now was a little help from my friends. With this in mind I set up a Facebook Group and invited everybody I could think of! Soon the word began to spread and I received submissions from all over the UK and as far afield as Israel, the USA, India and New Zealand. Some of these people, most of whom I do not even know, have moved me to tears not only with their poems but by opening up their hearts and sharing with me the true stories behind them. My heart goes out to every one of you who has been touched by cancer in some way. We never think it is going to happen to ourselves or our loved ones but, sadly, it does.

At this point I decided to approach a few high profile poets and the response was fantastic. Ronnie Goodyer of Indigo Dreams also introduced more poets and negotiated permissions through his many contacts, and it is this broad church of first-time published to the internationally famous that we believe makes the book so special.

I feel truly proud to be part of this collaboration of people who made this book happen. Thank you all.

Annie Morgan, Co-editor

Macmillan Cancer Support

Each day 822 people in the UK are told the devastating news that they have cancer. Macmillan Cancer Support aims to improve the lives of people living with cancer, as well as supporting family members, friends and carers. Macmillan's increasing range of services, include nurses, doctors and other health professionals, cancer care centres, specialist cancer information and help with finances.

Right now, Macmillan are only able to reach one in two people who need this vital support. It is their ambition to be able to reach everyone. All of these services are only possible thanks to people's generosity and every penny raised by the sale of Soul Feathers really will make a difference. The publishers have waived profit to enable its retail price and for every copy of Soul Feathers sold £1.38 (Inclusive of VAT) will be paid to Macmillan Cancer Support (Charity Registered in England & Wales (261017) and in Scotland (SC039907))

If you have questions about cancer you can contact Macmillan on 0808 808 00 00, or visit www.macmillan.org.uk

About Ronnie...

Ronnie Goodyer ran a celebrity management company for a number of years and, among others, published Uri Geller's first novel, 'Shawn'. He introduced poetry to publishers Bluechrome and, as their Poetry Editor, gave many new poets their first chance of publication, devised and selected work for anthologies and adjudicated their competitions. He left Bluechrome to form Indigo Dreams Publishing, now limited by guarantee, which he now runs with partner Dawn Bauling.

They publish three successful poetry and prose magazines, anthologies, collections and fiction. Ronnie is an experienced poetry adjudicator and in 2009 was selected as a panel judge for two locations in BBC's 'Off By Heart' poetry series for children. There are six collections of his own poetry.

CONTENTS

13

15

SOUL FEATHERS

Gesture – Carol Ann Duffy

Did you know your hands could catch that dark hour,
like a ball, throw it away into long grass
and when you looked again at your palm, there
was your life-line, shining?
                          Or when death came,
with its vicious, biting bark, at a babe,
your whole body was brave;
or came with its boiling burns,
your arms reached out, love's gesture.
                              Did you know
when cancer draped its shroud on your back,
you'd make it a flag;
or ignorance smashed its stones through glass,
you'd see light in shards;
paralysed, you'd get up, walk;
traumatised, you'd still talk?
                          Did you know
at the edge of your ordinary, human days
the gold of legend blazed,
where you kneeled by a wounded man,
or healed a woman?
                      Look-
your hand is a star.
Your blood is famous in your heart.

Good morning world – Dorit Weisman
(written the morning after the operation)

Good morning hummingbird on top of the eucalyptus
good morning sound of a distant car
good morning radio station
good morning hammock
good morning Dr. Zamir who asked me "What kind of
computers do you work with?" and when I said "Big ones" he said,
    "Move them one at a time"
good morning sleeping people whose minds are awake and to those
    who are awake with sleeping minds
good morning operating room staff who let me listen to music with
    earphones
good morning people in green scrubs and shoe covers
good morning bright lights and nickel surfaces in the operating room
good morning my body which is peaceful, at ease and not in pain
good morning breast cancer sister , who suffered terribly in the
    recovery room, good morning sister, I don't know you but
    you're still you, you'll always be you, two breasts or one

good morning smiling nurse Ilana who bid me goodbye, her bag on her
    back
good morning all the nurses I can't remember
good morning left breast,
good morning right breast too, I never knew you were that big
good morning t-shirt
good morning nipples and smooth skin
good morning smooth skin of my thighs
good morning samples of my flesh cut stained examined, good morning
    may you bear good tidings
good morning my extracted tumour
good morning clean body and benign blood flow and all my healthy
    cells
good morning plasma and lymph and lymphocytes and thrombocytes

good morning my smiling face
good morning writing hand
good morning this red red geranium
good morning garbage can
good morning old round heater
good morning plastic chairs and awning
good morning pleasant breeze that strokes all my pores and to the
    stronger wind that suddenly blows across my hair and to the
    shampoo waiting for me in the shower.

Mother Harvest – Jim Carruth

(i.m. Margaret Carruth 1938 -2008)

Mother forgive me these last few visits.
Before it is too late I have come

to support again your painful shuffle
as if barefoot over a stubble field

to harvest your every smile, your love
for others, your hope for all

our futures, to gather in each precious word
stack more carefully in my heart-barn

your deep tone of casual conversation.
Seed your half-forgotten memories in mine:

the child sprouting from Ayrshire clay;
the adult on the hill working the seasons.

All these and more I must reap to feed
the hunger in my remaining winters,

these rushed short days with you
bringing in the bales before the rain.

An Aspiring Spirit – Derek Mahon

after Quevedo

The final dark can take away my eyesight,
obliterating the white blaze of day;
it can release my soul and maybe gratify
the anxious hope of an eternal light —

but even on the farther shore it won't deter
the thought of where my earthly being burned:
blithely ignoring the strict rules, my fond
desire will swim back through the icy water.

The life that held such an aspiring spirit,
the arteries that fed so much impatience,
the marrow once so glisteningly bright

may wither, but their ardour will survive.
There will be ashes, yes, but smouldering ashes;
there will be dust, but dust glowing with love.

'An Aspiring Spirit' from *An Autumn Wind* (2010) by Derek Mahon by kind permission of the author and The Gallery Press, Loughcrew, Oldcastle, County Meath, Ireland, from An Autumn Wind 2010

Hope – Keki Durawalla

One evening we saw a rose coloured cloud,
                              but what of it?
We have watched the overhang of rain
one lunar fortnight after the other
metamorphose into flood,
and we've let the memories of drought disappear
unnoticed. We've seen both rain
and the long hot days of not-rain, when even
shadows seemed to fry on the braziers of brown sand.

Yet beyond brown fretful river and brown
simmering sand there was always a strip of light
at water edge and the other side of the heat haze.

Father left me with a painting called 'Hope'.[1]
She squats on the globe blindfold
with a tattered lyre—just one string left
her back bent, her ear glued to the lyre,
to the one chord of the downbeat lyre.
The earth-globe on which she sits, hunched
is dark but for a mild glow near her feet.

Her raiment is thin, translucent
but the whole effect is ethereal
and there's hope, for as long as there's
melody in that single chord
and you're left with a finger
to strum it with, what's there to fret?

The rose coloured cloud may not alight on land
poverty may not don radiant robes
herrings won't give birth to goldfish
but mystery and wonderment will
await you at some corner
and future is the site, where some day
innocence will set up camp.

[1] The allegorical Painting 'Hope'(1886) by George Frederic Watts

Can't Cook, Don't Cook – Steve Allen

I don't cook.

I eat raw.
I eat healthy.
I *heat*.
I eat 'microwave'.

Six months after moving house,
I used the cooker for the first time.
Three years later,
I discovered it has a grill.

I don't cook.

But with you listless in bed,
off solids for days,
I came and worked for 90 minutes
in your kitchen.

Following your favourite recipe,
I peeled,
I chopped,
I cubed,
I boiled.

I used that blender thing,
to make butternut soup.

Delicious, you said,
as surprised as I was.

It's the way it's made.

From *Tasting The Fruit* – Indigo Dreams Publishing 2010

Taste of honey – Moira Andrew

From the beginning

our dark was like
a hive of bees, murmurings,
the beating of wings.
We lay at the cross-roads
of night, dreams making
a bee-line for morning.

From the beginning

our joy was a talisman
against the backlash
of time. We tasted
honey on our lips, gossiped,
giggled, whispered, even
our silences were sweet.

From the beginning

we knew the end
was close, but veiled
the truth with *I love you's*.
And when it came, with
its sudden sunshine sting,
we were still candy-kissing.

From *This year, next year* – Marvin Katz Press

Flowers – Arthur Rimbaud

From a golden step,-- among silk cords,
green velvets, gray gauzes,
and crystal disks that
turn black as bronze in the sun,
I see the digitalis opening
on a carpet of silver filigree,
of eyes and hair. Yellow gold-pieces
strewn over agate, mahogany columns supporting
emerald domes, bouquets of white satin
and delicate sprays of rubies,
surround the water-rose.

Like a god with huge blue eyes and limbs of snow,
the sea and sky lure to the marble terraces
the throng of roses, young and strong.

Candlemas Bell – Oz Hardwick

They said she came to soften the Fall,
feather-white on hard fields, frozen
days giving way to warmth, a promise
that nothing but kindness will last forever.

A comforting thought for those who believed,
but now confined to dog-eared books,
quaint antiquarianism and cul-de-sacs
of the internet, stumbled upon by chance.

Yet, as winter tips imperceptibly
to longer days, she comes again,
lifting her glass to parched lips,
saying nothing, promising all.

This Is My Body – Tessa Ransford

Cut to the heart I hear
the woman behind the curtain beside me:
'Thank you doctor, thank you.
You are most kind I know
you saved my life by cutting off my breasts.
Excise now what you think best:
my ovaries, the left breast?'

In our humiliation and mutilation
we do not question that he has
our individual good at heart,
rather than his research, beneath
his wholesome white-coated front.

He parts my curtains. I refuse all
to be on the safe side further operations.
Amazed he shrugs: 'It's your body.'
I know it is. I choose to choose my treatment.
He warns I will regret it. *So he knows*
What's best but still continues the research.

I stick to my guns – a phrase by which he means
I do not go along with his proposals.
I vow no more drugs. No more needles
probed in my already-gashed breast.
In tears of doubt I am dismissed.

From *When it works it feels like play*, Ramsay Head Press, Edinburgh, 1998

(Author note: Delighted to say things have improved since this poem was written)

30

Heartfelt – Jan Harris

At the centre of my heart I found

a sorrow, loosely wrapped in tissue,
the shape barely visible through folds
arranged to soften the sharpest edges;

a need, locked in a crystal box,
un-met and undiminished, glowing softly
for those who care to see;

a hope, cradled on a velvet cushion,
to be handled only with white cotton gloves,
sheltered from public view and interrogation;

a mystery, fully sensed but only half known,
hidden by screens of self-deception,
clearly elusive and apparently untouchable;

a joy, which will not be contained
and sometimes soars unbidden in clearest view,
but usually nestles quietly within;

a love, stored in many different moulds,
nurturing, passionate, unconditional, fragile,
all stacked and labelled for daily use;

a choice, to open the door to my emotions
and live life to its turbulent extreme,
or to remain a jailer to the secrets of my heart.

Our Daughter, The Bible Flasher! – Daljit Nagra

...but you must our daughta cure Dr Jekly!
Spells by wife is mek daughter worse.
I tell of how it start: at party for full moon
di girls is whooping wid broomstick dance
and wise-hair ladies gassing voodoo-powders
in corner. I leav di Bacardi guggling
Bernand-Manning-to-Edingborough-Duke
joke-cracking boys who mek di *haha, ah!*
In hallway I see a girl twitchey her nose.
O Dr Jekly, it our Rapinder, her sari –
tutt-tutt-tuttering to lino!
                              Underneath
she hav white collar and black costume!
Wid eyes to ceiling artex, wid bible she march
for marquee, screeching like dis (I sing):
All tings briiiiight and beauuuuuti-
pelll, di God-lord changing allllll...
Such jumble, Dr Jekly, she mumbo, so quick
up I roll her to play wid Black Magic masks
in attic. And ask, *Vut is wrong wid Rub?*
Always, again in British on me:
Does he too do Christmas making money
for charities with Cliff Richard?

'Rub' Punjabi word for 'God'

The Queen Of Santa Fe – Dylan Harris

My memories are slippery and sharp,
and coloured by the heat of her,
adventurous and sweet.

Three months ago, I met the Queen of Santa Fe,
her hair as red and long as twenty seven years.

She caught my English words,

her throne and duty may have been this city in the dust,
but she'd never left her Isis home,
a council youth, a river bank,

a teacher with the petulance to force a lifetime long–haired girl
to cut her pride, to mark the drought of '76.

She heard my English words

and spoke, exuberant,
compleat of drink and desert glow,
she spread her history.

She kept my English words,

and dreamt her night in Oxfordshire,
as snow touched down on foreign lands
where she will ride forever.

Our light fantastic – Andrea Wren

In ripe cherry rapture
I picked a sugar-spun star
from the sky that we shaped,
when we created the world.
My hand tingled as I pulled,
a radiant wave of rhapsody
pulsating through fingers and bone,
hairs prickling as if miniscule crabs
were nipping a pathway to the sea.
It beamed pink and rainbow in my palm,
sweetly beating heart
of a Crayola factory.

Bathing in colour that was ours,
we were whirlybugs waltzing in its glow,
light as spidery silken thread.
Caught in a hypnotic hue,
we danced until dizzy,
like thieves who'd fleeced a Fabergé egg.
And, as the star's shine
slowly dimmed to a shimmer in my hand,
astral body crumbling
into day-glow dust,
we looked to the sky again,
and it was your turn to pick,
from that infinite, celestial trust.

This poem is dedicated to my friend Dug McLeod and his late wife Ally

Kew, Richmond, Jane – John Greening

I had entered the mausoleum and searched
in the gloom for our name, and held the casket
that no one had touched for forty years,

then followed the river from Occupation Road
along past the Botanic Gardens
to Richmond Bridge. I had climbed the hill

and reached the kissing gate, though the sky
threatened above the Star and Garter, above
the 'Murder - Information Wanted' placard

on the Terrace Walk. I had called Mum
who told me they were on that very spot
the day Dad's mother collapsed

and you were born in Dar. I had found
our favourite haunt, the Café Mozart,
playing Arab music, and was just

repacking my rucksack off Paradise Road
when a stranger, courteous, eastern
accent, stopped and stared at me

and said: *You are a lucky man.*
I looked up at him. *Your face –*
it is a lucky face. I am fortune teller...

and he smiled and walked on past the cancer
shop, my thank you dropped after him
like a coin to that Big Issue seller

I had just ignored. A lucky man.

From The Silence – Jolen Whitworth

If he left no muddy footprints
on his mother's spotless floors
or crayon marks on the chintz,
it wasn't because he was invisible.
When he trembled at each peal of thunder
and campana of bells, it was with
excitement and expectation, not fear.

The arcane became his dulcimer,
a sounding board of spirit.
He appreciated the symphony
played out between the strings.
When disease tried to steal his voice
he learned to sing in a key tuned
to the guardians of silence, who
leave no wounds upon the soul
or the budding blades of tomorrow.

His footsteps echo down corridors
of a universe so harmonious
that even the deaf may follow
if they would but lend an ear.

Journeywoman – Alison Michell

I hadn't planned to go travelling
when – without warning – they sent me
on a journey to a land with no maps.
Sometimes I go on foot, climbing
slow stairs to the top of towers.
On other days I find myself blurring
through stations with unreadable names.

The lack of a guidebook disturbs me
at first. I want to know my destination,
time of arrival, will there be a bed?
But I've grown to like the unexpected:
a butterfly resting on a blue-painted door,
a walk on sand and seagrass.
Once I saw an eagle soar.

Somewhere the Other Side of Tomorrow – Max Wallis

Reading this
your smile's been stolen by a shadow,
winterstitched dressed in sorrow,
plastering pain over compassion.
Your shoeshined eyes all buckled-dull
in a monochromed world
in a knowhowwhen
somewhere the other side of tomorrow.

Listen.

I've been you.
Broken, in a greylit youth
know it's hard when you feel so young-old.
Lost. Timecracked, out of place
Wishing!
that PVA glue, sellotape and coffee
could fix all.

I was there,
snapped, drowning in a pub where everyone's talking,
hearin nothin, thoughts bee-buzzed frightening.
Down-stared, scared.
Limbs lift through treacled air.
I know phone-call-crying
bedboundtearshaking.
Ball-curled
five-am crawling outside parents' door
bunged up, phlegm-full,
life-sucked greygrimmed.
Trying to hold it in.

It's hard to remember me,
ginful, gay and gleaming.
Starshine.
You feel eclipsed.
But laughter rings through time, space, years.
All that dancing, daylight, jokes
and a thousand neverletmego hugs.
Bottle them, keep them.
They're ours.

Remember this,

in CCTV footage archives,
and thousands of tagged photos,
drunk, flashing, kissed and kissing.

In everyone's memories, forgotten hangovers,
gumption
and a million phone conversations
never written down
you're shoe-clad life-loved grinning
soulwinged and full.

I'm smiling now for you.

How to Suss Out the Night Staff – Catherine Graham

Ward 1

Do not ask anyone
who only smiles with their face:
They are on auto-pilot.

When you need iced water in the night,
ask the one who sings
Beach Boys songs to herself in the kitchen.

Join in:
Bar Bar Bar Bar Barbara Ann . . .

Harmonise:
Bar Bar Bar Bar Barbara Ann . . .

Then, for you are now best friends:
'Any chance of a top-up?'

Rockin' and a reelin' Barbara Ann
Bar Bar Bar Barbara Ann . . .

Day's eyes – A C Clarke

blink open
stretch out their petals
for a touch of sun.

We never catch
them moving
in the gap

between attentiveness
and attentiveness
see only now

how thick as snowflakes
they whiten June grass
which moments ago

stretched monotone green.

The heart does not break when bones do – Valerie Laws

My heart used to beat in the swift,
sharp tap of my high heels,
pecking out the rhythm of my blood. Now
heart and feet are out of step,
out of tune: my halting, muffled feet
pluck painful notes, to the percussion
of two sticks; a patter of uncertain rain.

But the heart does not break
when bones do. It holds firm
at the core, sound as an apple,
candid as a barn owl's
heart-shaped, apple-slice face.

My heart still hammers out the powerful beat
that used to find expression in my feet.

A Rare Ear – Sarah Hymas
after Les Murray

Distance may be reduced by knowing both places.
But for the one left behind, it's long range.
The detail's thin.

A bat flits, tufted in the darkness, turning on one wing
to cut away, as if into smoke,
gone.

Then back. With another. And a drumming,
a wooden bubbling, that isn't a desperate heartbeat, but
intermittent. I hear. I hear it.

And so, could I hear you? Five thousand miles further
than this black flame that can't be extinguished.
My sonar flickers like unanchored anger lashing out,

or love listening for its echo, a landing strip,
heard in the language of a kiss.

Versus – Miles Cain

The plump bag of Saline
steadily wrecked itself,
its liquid limping through
a tube towards my arm.

I ran a hand over my
freshly smooth head,
felt the strange downy hair
gather at my neck.

The man with looming shoulders
said it had taken
a trip around his body.
The shriveled look. The fight.

A gang of relatives,
crowded the ward
one summer night
like dark and silent crows,

eyes and ears
mourning conversation.
I slept and lived again,
walked into days
less numerous than cells.

Finding Out – Jo Heather

My survivor son lives
a long way off.
Today the weather map predicts
it will be raining where he is.
Here, cool April sun,
a day for being
outside, hyperactive.

I have hacked branches, and planted
the springy young lavenders: I will take
better care of these. I have sliced out
dandelions and bittercress. And puzzled
over the sudden ground elder:
a dragon's teeth seeded
through the underworld.

Today my survivor son has travelled
hand in hand with his beautiful friend
to the difficult place
where he will joke, she will try to smile,
as careful people slide him,
shadowed, radioactive,
into the light.

From *Knowing the Dark* – Indigo Dreams Publishing 2011

Love at Livebait – Gillian Clarke

for Imtiaz and Simon

That time she stepped out of the rain
into the restaurant, and suddenly I knew.
Beautiful in her black coat,
her scarf that shocking pink
of fuchsia, geranium, wild campion,
and he at the table, his eyes her mirror.

She said she didn't know then -
but the light in her knew,
and the diners, the cutlery, the city,
the waiter filling our glasses with a soft
lloc-lloc and an updance of bubbles,
and the fish in their cradles of ice,
oceans in their eyes,

and all the colours of light in a single diamond
sliding down the window to merge with another.
Later, saying goodnight in the street,
they turned together into the city and the rain.
On the pavement one fish scale winked,
a moon bright enough to light half the planet.

From *A Recipe for Water* – Gillian Clarke - Carcanet 2009

The Dolphin – Rowena M Love
for Insa

Cancer's a queer fish:
anaemic amoeba endlessly mutating;
puffer-fish growths bloated with poison;
or shoals of cells
that prowl like piranhas
stripping my health in their feeding frenzy.

But attitude can attack back,
till I'm the dolphin swimming free
from this sea
of sickness.

I'll trawl my system,
catching cancers and fears,
netting them to wriggle and squirm:
powerless.

I'm the dolphin swimming free.

Modern medicine may have me filleted,
canned and processed,
pumped full of additives –
but the rest is up to me...

I'm the dolphin swimming free.

Dread might dorsal my spine,
tears flood my face with brine
but I... CAN... DO... THIS...

I am the dolphin swimming free.

Crystal Walk – Adele C Geraghty

Remember when the magic was tangible?
Even before my eyes opened,
I knew it had snowed, for the stillness,
bringing the deepest of sleep,
of perfect protection and dreams
too mellow to breech waking.

Remember walking the streets on crystal clouds,
each crunching step echoed as if the only feet
in the world were your own? When the snow
made a silence; heart-stopping, profound,
the air so still, each whispered cry
was heard clear as a bell, for blocks around.

To say winter, to speak the word,
was to engage the magic, the word itself taking form,
a frosted breath. Faceted brilliance, balancing
light and aura, wrapping in a diamond raiment.
An embrace. Enfolding, slipping like a wraith
its icy freshness, through every crevice.
My lungs drawing in 'til it hurt, exquisitely.

The lace of a billion snowflakes
falling just for the chance to reach
the tip of my tongue, to have been created
only for this; to kiss my eyelids and lashes
for one sweet moment, before dropping like tears.
Remember how it seemed, for one night,
as if it should never end?

So even now, when endings are imminent,
I, It, Winter, become one.
I am the small crisp flakes, touching the ground
with a whispered sigh. I am each consummate crystal,
shed by clouds bluer than any eyes,
bursting a silver majesty to the ermine ground.
I'm there again, each time I see the small
clutching patches of white holding on for one more day.

Every time my feet make fragile, temporary,
frozen echoes, to be swallowed in millennia.
Each time I see the whirling, spun-sugar dances,
those fleeting, indecipherable traces,
I am home again, relishing every minute I have,
before closing my eyes for the melt.

Epitaph – Stephen Leake

I gave you the forest,
Full-leaved, carefully escaping itself;
Its carved secrets ringing in
The shrinking mouth of a lost bird.

You took it, direct as a prayer
The way a child receives an alien
Fruit, or discerning fly
Addresses a casual wound.

And we settled. Inseparable
Yet estranged in our sharp-shaped thoughts,
Dropping from the steps to
The muted absence of what lay ahead.

It was a place borrowed
Where we borrowed ourselves,
Warped in time's rumours.
With vines. Flint.

And you smiled across the
Interlude to a vanishing point:
A hint of verge where the white stone lay-

Its dreams still learning;
Its lyrics, grey.

She dreams of climbing a mountain – Joanna Ezekiel

She's packed an extra Mars Bar,
a bear-scaring bell, a kagoule, an inhaler
and a flask of champagne.
She needs the silence spread around her,
the crunch of stone and snow
beneath her hiking boots.
She'd like to stop and chat
to the mountain goat, ask his advice
on how to reach the peak,
where she'll plant her flag among
the neat rows of other flags
like lines of washing.
She needs to be giddy at high altitude,
to look down from the peak
to the thin blade of highway,
at its toy cars below.

From *Centuries of Skin* – Ragged Raven 2010

Breaking ice – Neil Reeder

The kitchen crackles
with oil-besmattered sausages.

His words surprise me.
They are friendly
and the silence has lasted
icily long.

My father's tone is calm,
a languid, almost purring baritone.

Trying to connect, we talk
of past Christmas's, cricket,
our family's past disastrous house moves

- and he hands me a peace offering:
slabs of bacon enveloped
in an aromatic pool
of smiled-on tomato juice.

Elspeth Owen's Bowl – Pippa Little

is hand formed from a coarse clay body
then burnished to pale ochre-green and cobalt's
soft greys, given a low firing
with shards, salt and seaweed;

some controlled cooling to assist the growth of crystals,
then glazes, poured, allowed to overlap.
Iron gives rich mustard, copper, moorland greens,
turquoise blues and oxbloods

burnished first at leather-hard stage then later, again,
with the back of a spoon. Now the whisper of your fingers
accepts from me this craft that will carry you away,
precious ship whose cargo and soul are one and the same –

feldspar, dolomite, bone, ash.

Westbury, October – Penelope Shuttle

Hang-glider over the white horse,
sun-lit rider,
gnat-small over the white tail,
flank, neck...

Green hillslope
displaying the horse,
as a green wall
holds a pure-white arras
of equine design,

a green so scarab-beetle bright
it has stopped believing
in autumn,
even though the calendar says
  October's almost been and gone

I'd give a lot to be the one
who wings it like a minor-dragon
over the chalk-carven horse,

to be held aloft in blue air,
skim-buffeting the thermals,
steering unwaxen wings close to the sun

who glides his rays closer day by day
to the closing stable door of winter

From *Sandgrain and Hourglass* – Bloodaxe Books

Animal Rescue – Antony Dunn

To say nothing of all the moths and wasps
I've been opening windows for;

the sheep headlocked in the wire
of a fence,

the newt in the slippery inch
of a dog-bowl of rain,

the spider coming off and off
its wall of death in the kitchen sink

and the bat flopping the living room floor
in a straight-jacket of dust, cobweb and hair.

I have angled your skulls
impossibly free,

poured you out into colour-matched weeds
at the edge of the pond,

offered you into a wineglass and out
to the forest of herbs,

and taken you into my own
unravelling hands and worked you loose

in this borrowed house; let you go
on the slopes by the buzzard tree.

Now, who is coming for me?

Chemistry Day – Pauline Kirk

"We are all formed from star dust!"
the lecturer says, displaying her picture
of Planet earth. Rocks, sea

tigers, ourselves, we are all
atoms of that exploding star raining dust
throughout the universe.

The boy chewing gum,
those giggling girls ... , myself,
we are all particles of star.

I need the odd reminder.
Wordsworth saw that spark of divinity,
though, years ago, and more clearly.

For him, birth was but
a sleep and forgetting, adulthood
a slow decay of vision.

With a teacher's tired eye,
I look round, and find it hard to think
the child divine. Yet one boy sits

transfixed, watching Eternity.
Near him, a girl clasps her hands,
imagining great discoveries.

The stardust shines still -
even in a Chemistry Lab.,
on a February afternoon.

Feather Books Collection number four, Feather Books, Winter 2002 (ed. John
Waddington Feather)
Owlstone, by Pauline Kirk, Thalia Press 2002 (ed. Lesley Quayle).
Gabriel, number eight, Spring 2009 (ed. Thelma Laycock)

Windfall – Claire Pankhurst

How long did it last
every sleepless early morning
red-rimmed dark sidling away
with just one backward glance
at the trees
sagging and bent over their burden
holding onto shadow
and green decay

until this morning
the sky tearstained grey
but the light
fingering its way through branches
sideways
catching the morning by surprise
and stroking away
the last remnants of night

and at first you think
nothing's changed
but then suddenly
a rush of years
and you remember old Molly
her cellar filled with damp sweetness
her fallen apple cider
her sadness, her smile

and the day unwraps a new moment
with this fruit in your hand now
under the trees' curtsey.

I dreamt of scissors – Kim Goldberg

I dreamt of scissors

I dreamt of lizards' tails falling off
in my hand

I dreamt of frantic wingbeats, frail cries,
anchored, tethered, flailing, failing
to rise

I dreamt of snipped attachments

I dreamt of unthreading needles wedged
deep in bristly hearts of haystacks

I dreamt of unfinished pancakes, unfinished
maps, unfinished engagements, unfinished
lives

I dreamt of a face with no eyes or nose or ears
or mouth or hair, just a bare egg naked and
waiting

I dreamt of letting go
of the branch

This poem first appeared in the author's 2007 book, *Ride Backwards on Dragon: a poet's journey througy Liuhebafa.*

NOTE: There is a Buddhist parable about a baby bird getting ready to fledge. The bird makes its way out onto the tree limb and is flapping its wings with all its might while squawking "I can't fly! I can't fly!" And the parent bird answers, "Let go of the branch."

Singular – Eleanor Dent

He knew he had been singled out for greatness
and so he told himself he shouldn't mind
if other children labelled him as "odd"
for frowning on their infantile behaviour
as though he stood apart from them, disdainful
of their prattle and their giggling and their sloth.

He knew that other peer-groups would await him
and so he bore the hurt of not belonging
and clung to his integrity with ardour;
a shabby little hero of the inkwell.
His masters voiced approval, but the praises
of those he prized and yet despised stayed absent.

He knew, his genius once become apparent,
that those who mocked him now would one day crow
about the days when they had been acquainted
conveniently forgetting cruel taunts
and they would fawn and simper when, by chance,
they met him, reminisced, and parted friends.

He knew his future would eclipse the present,
though he would find it easy to forgive
their envy, seeing him inspire desire
in glamorous women, mindful of their sneers
because he'd longed for more than transient pleasures
and waited, waited for a precious joy.

He did not know the depth of self-deception
he practised, for, if truth be told, he never did
amount to very much, and people always would
consider him as singular, and wonder why
he never made the effort to conform;
he might have been contented to belong.

From *Singular* – Indigo Dreams Publishing 2009

rebirth – Sue Johnson

on this first day of my new year
I walk through woodland glades
cracked with spring sunshine
wishing you could live for ever

I see the intense green of bluebell leaves
that you may not see flower
and I barely notice the path
starred with wood anemones
and white violets

a fox skull lies amongst primroses
and reminds me that no season is for ever
there is always death
before resurrection and rebirth

Dedication:
I'd like to give thanks for the work of Macmillan Cancer Support. This poem
was written for my late father Frederick Stephen Bloss who considered a
woodland to be his cathedral.

Dedicated To David – Michael Chapman-Johns

Love is powerful,
But only with you.
Cancer is dark,
And it has its eye on you.
Warriors in White,
Fight for you.
Out of the dark and into the light,
I walk with you.
God has my witness,
I'll never leave you.
Alone you're not,
Together we are,
Stronger than anything,
Nothing can tear us apart!

Find Me – Maggie Sawkins

In the ring around a blackbird's eye, find me.
In a cup of ocean, a patch of sky, find me.

On this the shortest day of winter,
in the persistence of a seagull's cry, find me.

In a blade of grass by a dusty roadside,
in the mating song of a harvest fly, find me.

In the huddle of trees outside your window,
in the moon's gaze and the wind's sigh, find me.

At the top of a blue stack mountain
imagine feathered wings and fly, find me.

As you cast your breath you'll find the answer
in the place where shadows lie, find me.

From *'Is it possible to write a religious poem in the 21st century?'* - Flarestack.

Fairy Ring – Linus Lyszkowska

Under the radiance of a silver moon,
A corps de ballet of pirouetting fairies
Danced lightly across the silvered lawn,
Scattering in merry elfin profusion
Countless tiny, fragile toadstools
In a perfect silvery fairy ring.

Step into the magical, mystical circle
Of a fairy ring,
Close your eyes,
Make a wish,
Know it will come true.

From *In Memory's Book* – Indigo Dreams Publishing

Her Gift – Sarah James

The gift of hope sits on the mantelpiece unopened.
Silver foil glints in the light, reflecting sunshine;
pink satin curves into ribbon smiles.

Small as a matchbox, her sister's parting present
weighs heavy as a wooden block in her hands.
There is nothing in it, of course – and yet everything.

The label's tiny handwritten italics tell her
'This present of hope is wrapped with care
and given with love, to be kept unopened.'

Her fingers curl around its solid edges.
Hugged snugly in her palm,
this is more than a symbol.

This sealed gift
shrinks thousands of miles of land and ocean,
reduces any distance to a promise she can grasp.

Autumn – John Stocks

Dordogne.

Then moonlight trembles on a cobbled yard
Where French girls stand, holding their bikes
Some smoke, struggling to find an easy grace
Chat softly, almost in whispers.

I stroll down some half remembered lane
Knowing I could belong here now
Sit night after night in the same café
Listening for the invisible sounds
Taking the language as my own.
Then tomorrow I would rise and gather
The ripest of October fruits
For it is late autumn; and I am blessed.

A Glimpse – Walt Whitman

A glimpse, through an interstice caught,
Of a crowd of workmen and drivers in a bar-room, around the stove,
late of a winter night--And I unremark'd seated in a corner;
Of a youth who loves me, and whom I love, silently approaching, and
seating himself near, that he may hold me by the hand;
A long while, amid the noises of coming and going--of drinking and
oath and smutty jest,
There we two, content, happy in being together, speaking little,
perhaps not a word

Your Hopes, My Hopes.....Our Hopes – Jumara Nazmin Akthar

Boy: "I hope one day I own an Audi, build my own house, have a holiday apartment in Greece."
Girl: "I hope one day we live comfortably, have picnics in parks, walk beaches in peace."
Boy: "I hope one day I travel the world, experience new adventures at each turn."
Girl: "I hope one day we have two children, doctor daughter, architect son."
Boy: "I hope one day I have a successful career, show my potential, put in place life plans that are clear."
Girl: "I hope one day they find a cure, your life is longer, and you are always here."
Boy: "I hope one day I can teach you to smile, show you how to be optimistic, forget that pride."
Girl: "I hope one day you realise, my darkness has gone, I am content with life with you by my side."

Girl:
"I hope day comes sooner than later,
So you don't keep pushing me away,
I hope one day comes sooner than later,
So I am in your life to stay.
I hope one day comes sooner than later,
So each of our dreams can be true,
I hope one day comes sooner than later,
So when I say I love you, you can tell me you love me too."

Sleep Suite – Sharon Olds

To end up in an old hotel suite
with one's nearly-grown children, who are sleeping, is a kind
of Eden. The one in the second bed
rests her head on two pillows - I did not know that -
as she sleeps. The one on the couch, under candlewick
chenille, has here and there as he turns
the stuffed animal his sister just gave him
for his twentieth birthday. I roam in the half-
dark, getting ready for bed, I stalk
my happiness. I'm like someone from the past
allowed to come back, I am with our darlings,
they are dreaming, safe. Perhaps it's especially like
Eden since this is my native coast,
it smells something like my earliest life,
fog, plumeria, eucalyptus, it is
broken, the killership of my family-
it is stopped within me, the complex gear
that translated its motion. When I turn out the light and lie
down, I feel as if I'm at the apex
of a triangle, and then, with a Copernican
swerve, I feel that the apex is my daughter,
and then my son, I am that background figure, that
source figure, the mother. We are not,
strictly speaking, mortal. We cast
beloveds into the future. I fall
asleep, gently living forever
in the room with our son and daughter.

"Sleep Suite" from *The Unswept Room* by Sharon Olds, published by Jonathan Cape. Reprinted by permission of The Random House Group Ltd.

Self-Portrait as a Smooth-Skinned Beech – Jenny Hope

But do you remember the tree? It overlooks
our childhood home like a lord. Watch me
as I slip my waist between its skin and raise my arms
in celebration of something yet to happen.

My roots twist like toes into the quarry's side.
I guess my position is built on trust.
I'd have moved me if I had been them, when they
might have noticed this skinny-ringed sapling

and perhaps thought what sort of trouble
a fully grown specimen might have caused.
But they hadn't built the house then.
This land was a half-forgotten quarry.

Their grandparents hadn't been born.
By the time they'd got their act together
I was already well-established. Sometime
in my teens, I lost the will for ears, preferring

the vibrations of my own kind. In my forties
I gave away my eyes, and in my seventies I allowed
the wind my voice having proved my actions
would suffice. I go by scent and touch and believe me

when I claim they serve me more than well
now I'm multi-limbed. I'm quite the crone.
Grey squirrels root through my hair for facets
of beech mast and I wear a pigeon nest up high.

From *Petrolhead* - Oversteps Books, 2010
Previously published in The Interpreter's House

Measure for Measure – John Owen Smith

For those of us just turning grey,
It sometimes seems a little hard
To see things go the 'metric' way,
Inch by inch in our back yard.

With Fahrenheit we basked at eighty,
Now it's thirty in the shade;
Seems to me you're always freezing
When you count in centigrade!

Old pence, shillings, weighty pieces
With us since Victorian times,
Disappeared, and in their places
Came the tiny 5p dimes.

Ten stone twelve was not so daunting,
Now I'm sixty nine kg;
Doesn't matter, I'm no fatter,
But it's bad psychology.

Think about God's little hectare,
As we contemplate our lot;
Has our maker lost his acre?
Goodness gracious, surely not!

But the pub remains resistant,
Still pulls pints to quench our thirst;
Scholars of the rough right wrist can't
Contemplate a change that's worse.

By Canute! Imperial days
Now wither, fade and die;
Foreign ministerial ways
Invade our history.

For those of us just turning grey,
What can we do to force a smile?
Stand firmly in progression's way?
Better be a Europhile!

David's Star – Ty Van Brown

Today,
my brother told me
something special.
A request:
that if he was reborn,
he'd like to come back
as a star.

A Star.

He's twelve.
Twelve tender years.
And wants to be
born again
as a star;
beaming
with lost wisdom.

It stopped me.

This clarity of youth;
raw beauty,
unspoilt.
Unsullied by fear.
Always dreaming.
Always gleaming.
Like a reborn star.

Tossing Coats – David Fraser

Nursery school, lilacs not yet in bloom.

He bobs a green metal fish by a wand,
in an afternoon rare glint of sun
with winter rain now gone.

Real fish with gold-knife tails
dart toward the shade beneath
the flat slate rocks he kneels upon.

Train cars, blue and burgundy
pulled by soot-black puffing engines
rattle past the wire-meshed fence.

He wears a smock, with an emblem of a frog
that all the others think is ugly full of warts,
but what do they know of fish and frogs.

He dips his metal fish,
feels a brisk breeze pick up
behind his bent unlit back.

He hears laughter from a wider world
sees older kids toss their coats
into the wind to make them fly.

Somewhere, Something – Shanta Acharya

We travel not to explore another country
but to return home fresh, bearing gifts.

Our lives the airports we fly from,
our bodies and souls, maps and compasses –
days the journeys we make,
past the continents we leave behind.

Surely there is somewhere, something
that justifies our coming and going?

Isn't that why we seek a sign from each other
of experiences worth dying for
as we commune with love under starlight
brittle with frost and the sharp taste of blood?

Let's fly free, not nailed to a mast;
see the universe with new eyes
not blinded by shadows that light casts.

From *Dreams That Spell The Light* – Arc Publications (2009)

Hope... - Brenda Read-Brown

...is delivered with each baby;
is the box round every diamond ring.
It fills the air when children sing.
Begin again! it whispers
to each drunkard who has slipped from grace.
It smiles from every lover's face,
and slouches at each student's side.
It takes you on a fairground ride,
swims by you out to sea;
it's the athlete's personal trainer,
and the artist's promised fee.
It straightens out the collar
of each candidate at interview;
it's born again; it's new
with each bar mitzvah, Eid or christening –
with or without faith, it's always listening.
Hope is everybody's friend;
it gives the high that never ends;
it is the lie that lights the dark
when it lurks in rooms of death,
its truth unsympathetic, stark:
we live, and hope lives with us
    in each dawn
        and every breath.

Eternity's Child – Sylvan Rose

As adults we harbour resentment.
We fail to forgive and forget,
While the tear-stained face of a child
Laughs, though the tears are still wet.

As adults we harbour desire
For money, possessions and power,
While the child's inquisitive mind
Seeks only the name of a flower.

As adults we harbour illusions
Of what we will one day become,
While today the child is a pop star...
Tomorrow can wait, unlike some.

As adults we harbour attachments
To people, and places, and things,
While the child, like a butterfly, dances –
So fragile, the strength of its wings.

As adults we harbour great knowledge,
Yet somehow lose sight of the past
When, as an innocent child,
We knew all the good times would last.

So cast out the adult within you
And smile while your tears are still wet,
And just as a child you'll begin to
Laugh, and forgive, and forget.

Lady At A Mirror – Rainer Maria Rilke

As in sleeping-drink spices
softly she loosens in the liquid-clear
mirror her fatigued demeanour;
and she puts her smile deep inside.

And she waits while the liquid
rises from it; then she pours her hair
into the mirror, and, lifting one
wondrous shoulder from the evening gown,

she drinks quietly from her image. She drinks
what a lover would drink feeling dazed,
searching it, full of mistrust; and she only

beckons to her maid when at the bottom
of her mirror she finds candles, wardrobes,
and the cloudy dregs of a late hour.

Translated by Edward Snow

Glitter and Glimmer – Jim Aitken

Frost sparkled on the dark pavement.
The early morning sky spread out
like a gigantic black canvas
and kept my eyes looking down.

But they did not stay down for long.
Oppression having to be faced,
I raised my head and looked, leaving
the diamond glitter at my feet.

And there, like shutters quickly drawn,
I saw a mere slither of moon
piercing the darkness of the day;
a glimmer of hope for the world.

Blank Canvas – Gabrielle Gascoigne

Let's paint this life in different hues –
saturated colours
chrominance full on.
Let's blur the contrast of black and white
to infinite greyscale
compassion-shaded.
Let's stand in the light of a new dawn's
enveloping brightness –
luminance bathing.
Let's grab the full spectrum with both hands
experience wholeness
through shattered white light.
Let's see the brilliance of well-lit truth
bring clarity of thought
to sharpest focus.
Let's feel emotion's myriad tones
from highlight to shadow
with hearts wide open.
Let's trust in the picture's perfection –
deft brushstrokes of beauty
enlightening love.

Expectations – David Slade

The selection in her drawer was not exactly
what she would have wished for the occasion.
Most seemed even greyer than the clouds
that chased each other past her bedroom window.

As he walked the last hundred yards towards the house
his thoughts moved as swiftly as the dry brown leaves
caught in the autumn wind. None would remain
in position for more than a brief moment.

The lacy black bra and matching briefs against pale skin
were the best she could offer to delight his eyes.
And of course he might not even read the signals
hidden in her eyes and her soft spoken words.

What is expected of me? he kept asking himself.
Was the invitation to a meal a subliminal message
or simply a kind gesture to a colleague, a friend
who clearly existed on supermarket quick meals?

Would the skirt and blouse with the button front
be OK? Would one undone button be enough?
Would the lights be too bright or their dimming
be too obvious? Before or after? A test needed I think!

The lights in the house dimmed, went out and dimmed again.
Is this the right house? Did I misunderstand again?
Is this the right day? Did I misread the signal?
Should I turn and go now? – Avoid the embarrassment.

Fresh Air – Dennis Locorriere

Curse the wind when it's in your face
Making it hard to see
Forcing your head down
Pushing you back
Stopping you getting where you want to be

But glory be to that very same breeze
Blowing to your avail
Moving you forward
Giving you hope
Blessing your course when it catches your sail

From *Whatever's Burning Now* – Dennis Locorriere, Indigo Dreams Publishing Ltd 2011

Everything Is Everything – Max Dunbar

It began, as these things do, with a splash of blood.

About a third of the stool was livid scarlet, barely discernible through the pinkish swirl.

He generally took a dump early evening, just after getting back from the uni. It was Friday today, Kiera was calling from downstairs, they had ordered in and were going out, they were due to meet the others in the Salutation in half an hour and he was shitting blood. He thought: this is not going to fuck up my weekend.

Kiera worked for the council, as a housing officer; they had woken up together at Glasto and since then it had been more or less golden. He told Kiera she looked beautiful, as he always did at this time of the week. He did not mention the blood, and over the course of the evening it slipped from his mind.

They met his uni colleagues in the Salutation and did a roster of Oxford Road bars. At times he perceived what could be a long term problem (he had this image of a nameless waterbreak in the good roaring oceans of this night) but there were friends he hadn't seen for years, he was paying for one drink in three, there were half-formed arguments and shouted conversations with strangers in bars.

Monday he spoke to a doctor he knew at the uni. The guy said: people don't get bowel cancer at twenty-four. Two bricks of Weetabix a day.

It did not happen again until, suddenly, it did. That summer they had taken two weeks' leave and travelled around Italy. Returning home, they had moved out of the houseshare in Whalley Range and into their own flat in Chorlton. He was a full project manager now, and Kiera had got an honorarium from MCC. Wednesday evening, and they had been eating Poppolino's pizza and watching the regional news. They were going to Kiera's high school reunion at the weekend and his girlfriend was worried about her weight. He told her that she looked around seventeen and weighed about a kilogram.

Most people's minds drift when they take a shit and he got to ruminating on the inoffensive past. When he thought of himself as a child nothing came except a sense of something unformed, a head bowed, at once alive in the town and without recognition of Victoria Square and the Needle and the municipal buildings. Suddenly he needed an identity, suddenly he needed to keep up with his friends, suddenly he needed to go to Liverpool to watch bands and not have to get the last train back; suddenly you are alone, and no one loves you, and yet there is a dark pleasure in this loneliness, and in locking yourself away to cry. At some point it all made sense, but this wasn't a secret you could hand down –

The doctor he spoke to the next day wasn't as relaxed as the uni guy had been. He recommended a scan. The appointment was in two weeks. Over those weeks he got wrecked, made love, worked, saw a couple of films and then he went to the clinic and found out that this long-term problem was actually just a short-term problem. Six months. At best.

By November he was in the MRI.

Separated from other beds by a plastic slash of curtain, within reach of a table cluttered with well wishes from the uni, from his friends in Leeds where he had studied and found himself, from his friends in St Helens where he was born and raised, and from the great intercontinental sprawl of his own family, he slept and read and puked and thrashed out the chemo. His hair had gone, in snarls and clumps. He lost three stone through his arse. He wore a colostomy bag. Over the last month or so the flood of visitors had reduced to a stream, then a drip. He needed only Kiera, and she was in daily.

It was on one of these nights that he thought about converting to Christianity. His attitude to religion had been derisive, when his bowels were clean. But faith offered what nothing else could: the possibility of continuation. In the end you have no choice but to delude yourself. I am not strong enough to resist this temptation when the pistol is at my head. Yet in early December his thoughts swung from death to life. How little impression we make on the world; like stones skimmed across water.

And yet the only regret about his life was that there had not been enough. But can you ever get enough, really? If you leave nothing behind but a few Excel spreadsheets on the shared drive and a few stories told in Oxford Road bars and some fading memories and emotions in the heads and hearts of those that loved and knew you – was the whole thing just a waste of time?

What he could have told them was: it feels like sleep. And sleep is good.

By he was beyond talking: by the night of December 19 he could make sounds but no real words.

The warm weight of Kiera's hand in his palm was good and she was saying things and that was good. But she looked upset. What could possibly upset you? Don't you love to sleep?

It was like when you crash out in the middle of the afternoon after a heavy night in Hyde Park: pushed down into the mattress by strong, kind arms. In Hyde Park, in the afternoons, we used to walk through the shadows of the trees and have a pint at the Drydock. The chemistry that makes your body and your thoughts and your impulses and your memories and your emotions becomes the chemistry that makes the world. Tipping over from something into nothing, he could still hear Kiera's voice. Everything is everything, he thought. We'll be together in the springtime. And the sun will shine.

Lourdes – Maggie Butt

We are voyeur-tourists, greedy for miracles:
sniffing round the edge of pain; smirking
as nun in boiled-sweet mac raises her mobile

to photograph the statue of the Virgin; pointing
at coach-loads filling gallon cans with holy water,
a thousand candles guttering for profit.

Until in mass-raised voices I smell prayer,
the tang of it sharp on the tongue, sweat of it
naked in the air, and shocked by recognition

(it tastes of love, and so of course it fells
you to your knees) I see, weaving amongst
the crowd, hope threads on rainbow feet.

The Enduring Gene – Ralph Windle

We come of earth, of ocean and of sky.
Drop this one stitch, some skein of time unravels.
We are the needle's necessary eye
Through which the life-thread, past to future, travels.

Ours is the gene that cannot be ignored,
That bends the warp of Fate's incessant spinnings;
Refreshes meaning in the tired word;
Explodes all fraud of endings and beginnings.

Of music still to come we've shared the making,
Earth's restless anthem in which all are singers;
At every dawn and new-tomorrows' waking
We are to newer fruits the pollen-bringers.

Nothing's to come in which we lack all sharing.
Some echo ineradicably lingers.
Each life's particularity of daring
Informs these patterns at our children's fingers.

Survival tactics – Christine De Luca

You have retreated
into the singularity:
imploded into a deluge
of inexistence.

Out there are days:
tomorrows whose weights
are beyond lifting. Somehow
even yesterdays are relative,
have lost their focus, their reality.
There is only an interminable now.

The catalogue of things we do
looks long and burdensome.
There's little point. You're through

with words picked up and strung in sentences.
They cannot express this dearth of future.
They are too heavy anyhow:
heavier than silence. But now

at last your voice is lighter,
lighter than for months.
You lift the smallest skylight on your world:
ask me how I am, and when I'll come.

I sense the dove you sent out
has brought back hope, a slip of greening.
And that you've held the singularity
in your sights, and blown it free,
dared to stare future in the face
and once again believe.

Wast wi da Valkyries, Shetland Library, 2007

Bones – Hannah Sullivan

In the tar pitch beginning
creatures were born
from nothing.
Nothing shifted
when the soul of the dark
was born.
Something rippled.
That was that.

And light became
because dark cannot ripple alone.
Neither could move without the other
and there was air.

Beings came forth
and took shape
and it began.

According to the book
every tale starts with a beginning
travels to the centre
and journeys to the end.
Concludes.
And we all move on.

What if no one knows how?
The book
goes back on the shelf
the last words unread
the fire cannot burn out.

There is always more
wood
or paper
or blood
to burn.

Finish? End? Final?
Complete completeness.
The middle. The inbetween.
The wet
flesh ....
Wood burns
the air around my hands
and the smoke stings my eyes.
This is now.
Life.

Rewind.

The race of life – Maria Gornell

I was always running (away)
from self
for cover
fleeing the essence of I

Running from past
sprinting from future
giving the present a run for its money

Running like coward
or a bull dragged by its angry horns.

Running into dead ends
one way stop signs
forced backwards into
my own erected walls.

Running in fear
from time
in thoughts; cradling attachments like bones

Truth too pure
self too damned
running and running
desperate to elude
this light inside.

Realisation came in revelations
I despised – truth dawned
running – never moving
frozen on spot

I saw my running was leading
nowhere
as I fled with fearful eyes
into a harsh reality.

Now I am running – running across fields
forward – full circle back into self

Running and running for dreams
transforming my illusions
of reality.

Running into the future
full speed I greet the gift
of the present

racing into the light.

This poem is about running for the 5k Race For Life in aid of Cancer Research
in July.

The Touch – Roger Garfitt

A finger of sun
in the fork of an ash
finds the green hearts
of the violets, so down-
cast from a late spring
they incline to the moss
they are rooted in,
all their sugars gone,
until the gradual touch
of the light, implicit,
insistent, cajoles them
and they cup open, greedy
as the Sheela-na-Gig, or
the flowers' Alexandrian
blue, the top two petals
pulled back to show
the cuckoo's shoe.

The cuckoo's shoe is a Shropshire name for the dog violet.

Whisper – Anne Stewart

A teaspoon lies idly by its cup.
The cup is thick and white
and wide as half a teaspoon's length,
Turkish coffee shining thick
and dark inside. Too rich to slick
back down the sides, it holds
the swirl of an unseen hand.

The hand that placed the teaspoon there
has changed its mind, moved on
to bigger things: a touch to comfort
a fretting child, please a lover, make repair
to a broken thing, stopped and taken stock,
gone on to lead a forgotten prayer.
The prayer is gentle. The thought is kind.
Its whisper reaches everywhere.

A teaspoon lies idly by its cup.
It's hauling light from everywhere:
the brassy shine of a pouring pot,
an unseen hand and all that lies beyond.
It's cradling the world and crooning
softly, whispering that everything
is going to be all right.

These Words – Michelle Sorrell

.iess, Eternai,   .tfelt, Heavc
    Overwhelming,   ,mise ,Powerful,
   ;, Heartfelt, Heavenl)   ., Open, Omnipotent,
  Promise ,Powerful, Enc   .ternal, Everlasting, Hear.
  Open, Omnipotent, Overwi   .ng, Precious, Promise ,Pow
 , Everlasting Heartfelt, Heaven   Helpful, Open, Omnipotent, O
us, Promise ,Powerful, Endles,, Eternal, Everlasting Heartfel
ul, Open, Omnipotent, Overwhelming,Precious, Promise ,Powen
al, Everlasting Heartfelt, Heavenly, Helpful, Open, Omnipotent, Ov(
ous, Promise ,Powerful, Endless, Eternal, Everlasting Heartfelt,
ful, Open, Omnipotent, Overwhelming, Precious, Promise ,Powerf
ial, Everlasting Heartfelt, Heavenly, Helpful, Open, Omnipotent, Ove
ous, Promise ,Powerful, Endless, Eternal, Everlasting Heartfelt,
"ul, Open, Omnipotent, Overwhelming, Precious, Promise ,Powerf
il, Everlasting Heartfelt, Heavenly, Helpful, Open, Omnipotent, Ov
us, Promise ,Powerful, Endless, Eternal, Everlasting Heartfel
', Open, Omnipotent, Overwhelming, Precious, Promise ,Powe
Everlasting Heartfelt, Heavenly, Helpful, Open, Omnipotent, (
Promise ,Powerful, Endless, Eternal, Everlasting Hea·
.en, Omnipotent, Overwhelming, Precious, Promise ,r
'asting Heartfelt, Heavenly, Helpful, Open, Omnipc
·se ,Powerful, Endless, Eternal, Everlastin'
.nipotent, Overwhelming, Precious, Pr·
'eartfelt, Heavenly, Helpful, Open.
·erful, Endless, Eternal, E·
·, Overwhelming, Preci·
Heavenly, Helpful
Endless, Eterr
·rwhelming.
·enly, Hr
'ess,
.lr
\

Hope Shines – Paul Verlaine

Hope shines - as in a stable a wisp of straw.
Fear not the wasp drunk with his crazy flight!
Through some chink always, see, the moted light!
Propped on your hand, you dozed-But let me draw

Cool water from the well for you, at least,
Poor soul! There, drink! Then sleep. See, I remain,
And I will sing a slumberous refrain,
And you shall murmur like a child appeased.

Noon strikes. Approach not, Madam, pray, or call....
He sleeps. Strange how a woman's light footfall
Re-echoes through the brains of grief-worn men!

Noon strikes. I bade them sprinkle in the room.
Sleep on! Hope shines-a pebble in the gloom.
-When shall the Autumn rose re-blossom,-when?

Pause on the threshold – David Wheldon

Pause on the threshold, self-still—
Do I look onward by recall?
Or fathom out the unremembered past
by progress? Self-still, on the threshold.
Here the pause. Do I look inside
to the blood upon the skyline?
Or outward in thought without words?
Do I speak to the heart beyond
the horizon? To the pulse am I dumb?
A world self-still. So clear. So new.

Redwing in the Yew Tree – Pauline Hawkesworth

Like bowls of ice-cream
dipped in strawberries;
three round-bodied thrush
with red-tipped wings
yellow and red striped
eye-markings are bouncing
amongst snow-blossom
soft as their feathers.

Both conjured themselves
from the same sky
presenting a tableaux
unimaginable this morning
when clouds were grey
and rain threatened.

An ambrosial blessing – Anne D Morgan

Rain drops glisten
On flowers and leaves.

A delicate blossom
Floats on the breeze.

The gift of rain
An ambrosial blessing.

Sweet harmony restored
Between earth and heaven.

Hitting the Buffers – Iris R Morgan

When you are told you have cancer
It's a terrible shock,
Your life is on hold, like stopping the clock.
It can't happen to me you say to yourself,
This is the thing that hits everyone else.
We all have our crosses and problems in life,
Our ups and downs
Our good times and strife.
A wake up call perhaps for some,
Life should not be all work.
Life should have some fun.
A tough time ahead to fight this disease,
We can't just take off and do as we please!
Be positive, confront it, don't let it win.
With family and friends' help you will conquer this thing.
The nurses and doctors are all on your side,
Doing their job with humanity and pride.
The reception received at Oncology too,
Is the warmest of smiles and a kind word or two.
With faith and strength and all your might,
Ian, the end of the tunnel is a shining light!

Dedicated to my husband, diagnosed in 2004, who won his battle.

No Truck With Electricity – Ruth Smith

My grandmother was afraid
of electricity. It came from a place
she called The Mains. Nothing
could stop it entering the house
live and full of volts; enough
to fork right through her when she sank
three metal pins in bakelite.
She, who could power a mangle
and raise dust storms
when she beat her rugs,
saw an end when, one by one
her neighbours waltzed with upright Hoovers
and let the juice run soundlessly
into their irons.
                                  She comes to me
when I'm left alone in this humming room,
arranged just so for a measured dose
from the machine. It knows me now
and twitters like a familiar, then cranks
itself to buzz and beam.
Above my head there's a muzzy print
of a tree in full blossom against
blue sky. It's meant to soothe
but that wouldn't wash with her.
She'd fidget and put it down to 'nerves'
but freeze when the lights went down
and call back the radiographers
before they'd even left the room.

After Surgery – Jenny Hamlett

I begin as the outsider

in a room
weighted down with daisies
staggering under layers
of sweet Alice
bursting with cross-bred oxlips.

Hope is an antelope
at the foot of the bed,
ready to spring away
at the first hint of danger

so I watch the windowsill
filled with get well cards
and let my husband's smile
lie here with me

in this room
holding sunlight like water in a glass.

From *Talisman* – Indigo Dreams Publishing, 2009

I Bless You, Forests – Aleksey Konstantinovich Tolstoy

I bless you, forests, valleys, fields, mountains, waters,
I bless freedom and blue skies.

I bless my staff and my humble rags.
And the steppe from beginning to end,
And the sun's light, and night's darkness,

And the path I walk, pauper that I am,
And, in the field every blade of grass,
and every star in the sky!

O! if only I could encompass all life,
And join my soul with yours.
O! if only I could embrace you all,
Enemies, friends and brothers, and all nature,
And enfold all nature in my arms!

Hope – Barbara Robinson

Painful, how do I paint painful?
Is it a rupture of the mind
or a searing of a thought -
the sad sundering of a soul
or just a careworn
aching of a stricken heart?

Is that the hidden answer -
the deep aching of a stricken heart?

For that's what I felt then;
a division of feelings warm to cold,
highs and lows divided,
emotions stirred;
from everything to nothing.

I painted painful
as a numb severance of hope,
but I was wrong.
Eden can be reclaimed....

quite swiftly as a sunrise;
a shining rainbow's edge
cutting the morning's yearning
to be reborn as a warm
contented breath of the future;

my soul kissed softly
by an angel's falling feather
brought silent words of hope
and it was my turn to fly.

I Go To A Game With My Vigorous Father – Todd Swift

I carry my father in hospital sleep,
Wake to light that devours things,
Each night a new drowning.

New summer air recalls old summers
When hand-in-hand, younger,
The live baseball stadium was there,

With its Expos players, and mustard.
Delected air, that food, now seem
As good as if pure Jesus came again.

Oh, that he would visit here to cure
Cankered layers that make bread out
Of any modest body. A body

Cannot keep up with all the jilt-jolt pace:
Science, that trying, changes in us –
Won't often be weighed down by

Too much mid-July-wheeling faith.
I feel levelling opaque bodies fold
One on one, as I have grown a son

From my father's negative-active cells;
And take that rapid son of his from
My smashed-open head – and hells

Gush down like Niagara, Victoria
And all geographic falls –
Those rich, long places. Vindictive nouns

Cultivate far inside my lovely Tom
Like fast bees that build white honey
From their nameless industry.

Comb my father's white hair
Where it was not aggressively shaved
For the scarring. But a game is saved

For his pitted memory. He sees
A white-dirted ball fly in blue air, a boy,
His own it may be, moving by his tall side.

Never Too Late – Attila the Stockbroker

(In memory of my stepfather, John Stanford)

My father died when I was ten
and when she'd dried her tears
Mum met you in the choir -
she'd known of you for years
I was so pleased when she told me
that she would be your wife
and I looked forward happily
to a new man in my life

But you were the classical singer
who thought rock'n'roll was junk
and I was the Bolan boogie boy
who soon became a punk
You were the civil servant
for whom everything had its place
and I was the left wing activist
out there and in your face

Yes, you were the 'head of the household'
and I was the stroppy kid
We wound each other up for sure
We flipped each other's lid
But later we both learned so much
and something new began
And here's a poem I wrote for you
You decent, gentle man

So I went off to my own life
Left you and Mum to yours
A few words about football
Then the sound of closing doors
But the passing of so many years
gave us both time to reflect
And slowly, oh, so slowly,
we forged a new respect.

When you were ill the first time
and found it hard to walk
I'd take you to the hospital
and we would sit and talk
It felt so right and normal
And it was such a shame
that it had taken all this time -
Both stubborn, both to blame.

'Cos you were the 'head of the household'
and I was the stroppy kid
We wound each other up for sure
We flipped each other's lid
But later we both learned so much
and something new began
And here's a poem I wrote for you
You decent, gentle man

When Mum came down with Alzheimers
Five years you cooked and cared
And we were round there every day
so many thoughts were shared
Your simple, honest loyalty
The vows you made, you'd keep
No longer the big boss man
Me, no longer the black sheep.

Then came that day in hospital
The end was near, we knew
You told me 'I do love you John'
I said 'I love you too'
You held my hand and squeezed it
Our eyes were filled with tears
The first time that we'd said it -
It took thirty-seven years.
Yes, you were the 'head of the household'
and I was the stroppy kid
We wound each other up for sure

We flipped each other's lid
But later we both learned so much
and something new began
And here's a poem I wrote for you
You decent, gentle man

It's never too late
never too late
never too late to say you love someone

And if it wasn't too late for me and John
Then it's never too late for anyone.

www.attilathestockbroker.com

Little Sparrow – Poul Webb

Speckled, the colours of doves,
time-laden paviors, polished
to a patina by feet, boots, wooden
clogs that fell apart long ago.

Edged by honey-coloured buildings
of stone, the snicket glistens
like a sinuous stream trickling
down the hill, steep as a stairway.

A cooling breeze teases the air,
ruffles the hair of a brindled cat
skittering between deep shadows
in the turning of the day.

There is a café near the crest
where a waitress in baggy pantaloons
and bejewelled sandals waltzes between
tables dressed in gingham shrouds.

The dark and cool interior
boasts a large majolica cockerel,
an armoire the size of a car
and a listless albino fish in a tank.

In a discreet corner Edith Piaf,
sporting too much rouge and lipstick,
sits silently opposite her lover,
nothing to say, full of regret.

It's . . . – Amy Neilson Smith

It's the fact that there's always internet dating;
It's having faith that tampax will one day be tax free,
That their adverts will one day be banned, for being
Crassly indiscreet, as will page threes and *Anne Summers*;
It's counting the days to three months, when the
Bump starts to show and you can scream your
Heavily suppressed delight to the world: freely;
It's crossing all fingers and toes and hairs and veins for
Your sister's three A's; it's sucking your polo slower than
Your brother, knowing yours won't break first; it's
Pulling that wish bone; it's holding that poor little
Rabbit's dissected foot, lucky for you, not for him;
It's that after the rain, always come puddles to play in;
It's lighting that candle in church, even though you
Know God's not there; it's kissing the envelope
Before posting; it's squeezing a hand to let them
Know your presence; it's saying a much needed prayer
To yourself; it's making that wish as you blow out
Your candle, it's making it for someone else,
It's seeing that candle you lit, in your mind:
Hours later, it's feeling its incandescent warmth,
It's telling someone else about it, passing this glow
Forward; it is forward; it is the touchable line ahead,
Above; below and behind have dropped off the
Radar; it's looking at you dressed in a sterile gown:
Grey, weak, being bathed down; it's seeing the
Drip, it's holding your hand, and your mind in tow,
It's hoping that you won't let go . . .

Yet.

Hope – Tom Raworth

less is without
as aim or clue
minus, a subtraction
but not of care

there as a chain
reaction spreading, full
through static gloom
sprout shoots of light

Our Future Within Them – Anne Cluysenaar

No language. No clothes. No country.
Human, yet not quite human,
a family seeking survival.
Ahead: unknown hills. Behind:
their home, enveloped in fire.

When I see a mere butterfly
setting out over open ocean
I think of him, of her,
of the child criss-crossing their trail.
No city ahead. No city
behind. But our future within them,
at risk from volcanic ash
filling (preserving) their footprints.

To us, this would seem a disaster.
They kept straight on. Not running.
Not giving up. Together.

From *Migrations'* - Cinnamon Press, 2011

Holy Well – Angela Locke

Here the saint's hand, resting on moss
Burned, not a brand
But new green growth
By pale stone above the waterfall

These things are holy
And bear our reverence with ease
Yet we only know them sacred
By their absence

In city streets
And in the brutal ruck of lives
We burn dark circles with our hands
Not blessing, but denying life

Yet we too could bring light to winter grass,
Blessing all Earth's store
Angels are singing the land's song
We will not hear

Exhausted, against the rock
I feel the healing echoes
Of their music…
'Find rest in this forgiving, kindly land'

From *Sacred Earth* - Pleiades Press 2001

Parabola – Luke Kennard

to a defamed friend

Everyone can relax when the satirists leave for their dachas.
All Summer we hypocrites hold laughable opinions,
bowls of change and nuts on our telephone tables.

Our guarded Spring sentiments uncomfortable,
the way yesterday's detritus feels in your pockets.
In the walled garden you tell me you are fine

with the domestic turning hyper-real: (A rock pippit
with a skillet in its beak bursts into aquamarine
filaments against the sky; an egg-whisk, on expenses,

betrays you.) What you cannot accept is that the itch
on your knee, the missing branches from the willow,
the gnat's flight path were fore-ordained before the world began.

'What if gnats flew in perfectly straight lines
which formed parabola?' I ask you, closing my novel.
'What if everybody's left knee had that exact same itch?'

Had I invited a monk for your instruction he might
arrive now with a red netting-sack of oranges wrapped
round the seat of his bicycle and you would continue,

'How can this place where the wallpaper
peels because I chafed it with a stepladder, [1]how
can this tiny ink blot on the sofa...'

The day seems to last beyond its means:
In the next city a famous neurologist succumbs to dementia.
The last light seems to come from horizon-mounted golden floodlights.

The plants just want to expand and they don't know why,
Like FTSE100 companies, like hair. If only I could build a tiny robot
to wander through my brain's lousy platform game. But that isn't it.

I'm so sorry you're hurting.

I spent the afternoon in junk stores. I found you 12 somehow
Unnerving coins and a sewing box from the old country
Where needles evolved differently and everyone kind was tortured.

That isn't it either.

So I will conjure for you two guides:
one with petroleum clouds gliding over his single,
beachball-sized eye, the other who outwardly

resembles an investment banker or leatherbound book
and reminds you in a voice like a well-polished glass
that there are things infinitely more pressing,

like having enough coathooks.

---

[1] At this point I would weigh in with a story about an external wall in Bibiena which my grandfather scraped with his Cortina fifty years ago and how the scratch is still there, that I have been and touched it – not terribly relevant, of course, and I'm interrupting the monk I invited for your benefit. I never could resist even the vaguest correlation, conversationally speaking, whether with friends or strangers (and it strikes me now that it's our primary means of social discernment: how seamless are his transitions? How apparent is his desperation to be liked?) for attention, maybe, or to say I exist! I exist too! I have a family! I scratched my own wallpaper! Some have died! I love! I love! And so the monk pats me on the head and wanders off past the wattle-and-daub shack, his hand trailing in the foliage – which is something I've seen already, but when I try to place it it recedes like a dream you thought you remembered, the way an octopus turns and vanishes.

After the Operation – Rory Waterman

And there you were: awake, propped on the bed,
head up, knees up, smiling from a book,
the ward eerie with calm.
I don't remember what it was I said,
Mum, but I remember that you looked

eager, like I'd not quite seen before,
your big eyes shining as I came across
to touch your cheek to mine,
as love and hope cut free your albatross.
And this was what you had been fighting for.

The Memory Of Water – Ian McDonough

In the quiet times,
snowdrifts high outside,
nothing comes to mind
but the memory of water.

Remember how it moves so
swiftly through the world,
and how its mirrored
surface holds your gaze.

How currents warm its
molecules, dissolve the
icy fissures threading
through your frozen days.

In the crystal times,
white and paralysed,
feel the itch of spring,
the alchemy of water.

Off Colour – Adele Ward

What should I do with this pain?
I can't sell it or give it away.
Should I hate this pain
for catching me in its arm lock
and forcing me to my chair?

Should I love this pain,
as perfect as birth,
as adolescence, motherhood,
each moulding their change?

Should I accept this pain,
feel how it forms like my own
infant hand, or hair pushing
endlessly from the roots?

Should I Google it, study it,
peer at it under a microscope,
marvel at its beauty, strange
and natural as a growth
on a coral reef?

Should I paint it in bright acrylics,
close my eyes and imagine it,
welcome it as the next stage
and part of me?

Behind closed eyelids, should I
look inside as its rainbow spreads
like dripped children's poster paints
bleeding into water?

When It's All Over – Myra Schneider

I'm going to throw open my windows and yell: 'halleluiah',
dial up friends in the middle of the night to give them
the glad tidings, e-mail New South Wales and Pacific Palisades,
glorify the kitchen by making sixteen summer puddings,
watch blackberry purple soak slowly into
the bread and triumph over the curved glass of the bowls.

When it's all over I'll feed my cracked skin
with lavender and aloe vera, lower my exhausted body into
foaming suds scented with honey and let it wallow,
reward it with a medal, beautify it with garlands of thornless roses,
wrap it in sleep. Then from tents of blurred dreams
I'll leap like a kangaroo, spout like a whale.

Once it's over I'm going to command my computer to bellow
'Land of Hope and Glory,' loudspeaker my news
down these miles of orderly streets where the houses wear
mock Tudor beams and plastic Greek columns, dance
the Highland Fling in front of controlled tubs of cockerel geraniums,
sigh with enormous satisfaction when I make the evening headlines.

When it's finally over I'm going to gather these fantasies,
    fling them into my dented and long lost college trunk,
        dump it in the unused cellar
          climb back to strength
            up my rope of words.

With acknowledgement to *Writing My Way Through Cancer* Jessica Kingsley
(2003) and *Multiplying The Moon* Enitharmon (2004)

Turn – Eileen Sheehan

As a poet
you need to be in love
with endings:

the soft turning
of leaves; the turn of the hands
of the clock;

a turn in the weather,
the return of early dark
to the evenings;

the turning away
of faces, turning
of backs.

Nonetheless,
on my walk to the graveyard
I plucked

a green caterpillar
from the pitted
road;

as a poet
you need to be in love
with hope.

Ffynnon Fair – Susan Richardson

Grief has led her here
in its hooded goatskin cloak,
with its crooked staff,
its cussed devotion.

She stutters
      down Grisiau Mair, each step
a slippery syllable on the stuck-out tongue
of cliff. The sea is a whip
that means to increase her suffering,
while Bardsey belongs to a bestiary,
hump-backed hulk, jaws frothing.

She supposes she should pray
but doesn't know the language –
and anyway, her voice is taut
as oxhide stretched
over a timber frame, unsteadied
by eddies of pain.

She turns, instead, to the well's whisper
of water, tinged
with a wish-glint of silver coins.

It will take more than one sip
to dispel her *accidie*
but already she can sense the squint
of a fresh beginning, the twitch
of a shearwater's wings.

Intercalary Days – Clare Holtham

For Ramez Kirollos

i.

It is that time of year: Halloween,
when the veils are thinnest
between this world and the next.

In neurosurgery, I'm under
for most of the morning. The surgeon
(trained in Alexandria) opens my skull
and lets in the otherworld. Anubis sits
and watches as he deftly separates
the pia mater from the dura mater.
The anaesthetists unravel the cryptic
crossword; the surgeon unravels
the deeper glyphs.

Later, Horus will perform
the opening of the mouth. Having scraped
the algae from the submerged face, divers
lift a stone head from the sea
in the Eastern Harbour: the green water
cascades from it; some forgotten guardian
of pity and terror, hauled up from the deep
in blindsight, blind like a fish from the abyss,
or a seer. A fathom down, the broken plinth
where a few Greek letters – alpha, tau, sigma
have lost their meaning. Just so the G,C,A,T
on the long arm of the chromosome: broken,
or scrambled in Cairo, half a decade back?

Cairo – the sky bled white by
an unforgiving sun, only tempered
by papyrus plants along the Nile,
and the bougainvillea in Heliopolis.

122

The taxi driver shows me
the City of the Dead: I don't want to stop,
I have questions to ask the Sphinx.
The shock of his stroke, his not being there
on the end of the phone, turns words
to ashes in my mouth; turns Cairo
to an unreal city, white and staring,
a daguerreotype over-exposed.

In the recovery room,
I try to sit up: I'm tethered right and left,
bandaged and stapled, bruised with two
black eyes: for a day and a night
I cannot see. I hear: bonfire night,
the drains in my head. The US elections
have come and gone, poppies
are worn for remembrance. Piece by piece,
the world comes back into focus:
I'm on a journey with Sven Hedin
across the trackless Takla Makan,
he is burying his dogs – and sometimes too
his men. I'm at sea with Jonathan Raban[1]
negotiating the inside passage,
trying not to be seasick.

At night
there is too much light,
the ward is overexposed.
I lie still, unsleeping.
I coast the shadow line,
bumping the shore.

ii

Orion rises over the village
bringing a blessed darkness.
I sleep, knitting the ravelled sleeve
of pain, but wake as the church clock strikes,
counting the hours, watching for morning's
dim but liminal light.

Friends help me wash and comb
my long hair, matted with blood
and staples. I breathe the country air,
tinged with woodsmoke, gathering my strength
like the wounded samurai in the film[2] by Kurosawa,
carried in a barrel to a hut in the graveyard,
there to slowly recuperate
practising throwing the knife
at a skittering autumn leaf on the threshold,
over and over again.

[1] Passage to Juneau
[2] Yojimbo

124

Prayer – Ron Butlin

When I reach the centre of the earth
let there be someone with me.
All things must bear the world's weight,
but not alone.

So when I return at last to this same hour
and this same place,
let there be someone raising even
the emptiness in their hands towards me.

If I Were Tickled By The Rub Of Love – Dylan Thomas

If I were tickled by the rub of love,
A rooking girl who stole me for her side,
Broke through her straws, breaking my bandaged string,
If the red tickle as the cattle calve
Still set to scratch a laughter from my lung,
I would not fear the apple nor the flood
Nor the bad blood of spring.

Shall it be male or female? say the cells,
And drop the plum like fire from the flesh.
If I were tickled by the hatching hair,
The winging bone that sprouted in the heels,
The itch of man upon the baby's thigh,
I would not fear the gallows nor the axe
Nor the crossed sticks of war.

Shall it be male or female? say the fingers
That chalk the walls with greet girls and their men.
I would not fear the muscling-in of love
If I were tickled by the urchin hungers
Rehearsing heat upon a raw-edged nerve.
I would not fear the devil in the loin
Nor the outspoken grave.

If I were tickled by the lovers' rub
That wipes away not crow's-foot nor the lock
Of sick old manhood on the fallen jaws,
Time and the crabs and the sweethearting crib
Would leave me cold as butter for the flies
The sea of scums could drown me as it broke
Dead on the sweethearts' toes.

This world is half the devil's and my own,
Daft with the drug that's smoking in a girl
And curling round the bud that forks her eye.
An old man's shank one-marrowed with my bone,
And all the herrings smelling in the sea,
I sit and watch the worm beneath my nail
Wearing the quick away.

And that's the rub, the only rub that tickles.
The knobbly ape that swings along his sex
From damp love-darkness and the nurse's twist
Can never raise the midnight of a chuckle,
Nor when he finds a beauty in the breast
Of lover, mother, lovers, or his six
Feet in the rubbing dust.

And what's the rub? Death's feather on the nerve?
Your mouth, my love, the thistle in the kiss?
My Jack of Christ born thorny on the tree?
The words of death are dryer than his stiff,
My wordy wounds are printed with your hair.
I would be tickled by the rub that is:
Man be my metaphor.

from *Collected Poems* – Dylan Thomas, reproduced with kind permission of Orion.

Poppies by Bosch – Wendy Webb

There is a piece of jigsaw
awaiting revelation, to the most misshapen poet
inspired by poppies.
Today, or tomorrow, the dove will descend
and all those pieces connect,
a work of art.

What Lies Beneath – Wendy Webb

It may be, there's a future I can't see,
to call you friend (though we have never met).
And you will find my words cannot be set
with ease; though they have heart and artistry.

It may take symphonies to understand
those quays to shades of light and darkest soul;
grown foreign notes of years I can't make whole,
to captivate a lost voice into sand.

My hourglass writ in water, splodged with ink
as nacreous as first love, seashell gleam
reflecting sun/sea/shore, where mermaids seem
material as scale-flash, wild airs' sink.

My life has been the storm of moon-tide drift
and, at their best, these sound-bites may uplift.

Damaged – Donald Adamson

There's not a single tree in the wood
that isn't damaged.
Yet they grow tall and old
and when at last they fall they are noticed
not by their malformations
but by their absence, sudden blue
astonishments of sky.

Being is its own achieving.
The fabric of things
mends in spans accomplished and the joy
of particular wounds. Do not ask to be cured
nor pass your parcel of injuries
to others. You were damaged, let yourself
be changed, and grow, and live.

(acknowledgement: Markings Publications)

Water Jug – Katherine Crocker

After the all clear, Mum cleaned the house.
She didn't want any possessions,
sorted out her cupboards, made us choose
from her hoards of treasure.

No question - I wanted the crystal jug.
It's something to remember me,
she said. Light poured on the glass facets
and a rainbow shone.

I could see her arms full of red rhubarb
she'd pulled from the clump
by the washing line and hear her scream
when the bee stung.

Then a candle-lit orange pumpkin
among the starbursts of fireworks
and how she laughed in the darkness
when Dad lit the bangers.

Yellow was the colour of warm olive oil,
poured in my ear when I was seven.
It dulled the pain of earache and the sound
of my head drumming.

Mum made green tomato chutney, hated
to waste the autumn's surplus.
So the family ate chutney all year round,
jars stacked high in her pantry.

Before she married, she satin-stitched
petals of blue daisies
and tiny French knots on white tablecloths
we always used for Sunday tea.

Her favourite tree was the plum, indigo fruit
falling among the hollyhocks
before the tree and house were knocked down
and they built the by-pass.

Every Mothers' Day, I used to pick violets
from the wooded bank at Clay Field.
I have years yet, but take something, she smiled.
I know. I'd like the jug, I said.

Hope For A Safer Place – Shelagh Watkins

When love shines through
In a world of little solace,
There's hope that honesty will prevail
Without fear of losing face.

If all children could be saved
From hunger and starvation,
There's hope they'd gain the strength
To build a stronger nation.

When all nations put down arms
And finally give up the fight,
There's hope for a lasting peace
If they could only unite.

As we become a nation
That doesn't hate because of race,
There's real hope that one day
The world will be a safer place.

Here Is The Place Where Loveliness Keeps House – Madison Cawein

Here is the place where Loveliness keeps house,
Between the river and the wooded hills,
Within a valley where the Springtime spills
Her firstling wind-flowers under blossoming boughs:
Where Summer sits braiding her warm, white brows
With bramble-roses; and where Autumn fills
Her lap with asters; and old Winter frills
With crimson haw and hip his snowy blouse.
Here you may meet with Beauty. Here she sits
Gazing upon the moon, or all the day
Tuning a wood-thrush flute, remote, unseen;
Or when the storm is out, 'tis she who flits
From rock to rock, a form of flying spray,
Shouting, beneath the leaves' tumultuous green.

I did not want for the grace of spiritual idleness – Sara Poisson

"La nécessité de parler et le désir de n'être pas entendu"
P. Éluard

I did not want for the grace of spiritual idleness.

A scorpion – an entire alphabet – twitched as if it were writing. Towers and turrets of ornaments, a beta of bees and an eta of kisses. A long path of signs, which once led to an effort to be.

A purple bird blossomed bleeding in a nest of salt. Everything rose as if descending and expanded as if fragmenting. Invented beings and crystalline non-beings spawned. I studied here, as though, chin in hand, you wanted to be and not to be my lover.

The blood was thick with tiny feathers. An ember held me between the sunset and the sharp contours of your shoulder, my love. In an instant, I saw a little feather reviving an ornament and within a second destroying. I saw it: a wrinkled hand, like an old glove, grabbing it. I don't know what affected my hearing. In shops, I heard dolls creaking in their cardboard boxes as they rolled over from one side to the other.

You told me graceful sentences are tedious, so I tried to mumble to myself si-si-si-silver, si-lver, si-vakadabra.

I had no tools other than being unceasingly quiescent about women's blood-stained wealth, about emulsions glowing above their bodies – she has no need to die for she is not yet born. I had no weapons other than talking about bodies, about colorful buckets in the grass so that you would leave my soul in peace.

I did not want for the grace of spiritual idleness. Spiritual idleness wanted for the grace of joy.

Now the pain in my head brings me joy.

Translated by **Ada Valaitis**

For A Friend Not So Far Away – Sean (TA-2) Gregory Buttram

In the darkness,
There was a light he could not see;
In the light,
There was a darkness in what he found;
Uncovering "true" beauty,
When it could not be found on the surface;

In the "I" of the Performer,
Beauty was uncovered in the tiny aperture,
The smallest little opening in his mending heart;

A ray of life...
A puzzle piece to a complicated story;
A light of truth...
A dream becoming reality;
Some stories when properly discovered...
Have happy beginnings.

In loving memory of James Key - a true inspiration

Blood-letting – Stan Hedges

When sorrow came you returned to the earth
to lie sidelong in the grass above a lake,
beneath an ash whose black mosaic leaves
played peek-a-boo with the light.
And it was then, after all the months of wishing not to be,
you discovered, at last, that man is of no greater value
than earth itself.

You envied the scurrying ants,
toiling incessantly, grumbling
at mere grains of sand;
while the lake below danced to
the sun's old song as it shimmered,
tossing kisses from wave to wave, until,
quite suddenly,
each glint stabbed you like a rod of truth,
remembering how the wise man said that
everything is in a state of simply becoming.

That lake danced with more joy
than you had ever known,
and you reflected in quiet mood until,
high above that self-indulgent acre,
a joyous lark intruded.
This last intrusion mocked your sorrow,
but you loved her still
for she knew no other way;
she never understood.

Ah, the things you never understood:
how meadows hum; how spinneys spin their spell;
how feathers float where there is no breeze;
how a breeze becomes a blow,
wind enough to set the cornfields pulsing,
wave enough to rock a mountain,
storm enough sink men's hopes.

Yes, you let natural wonders crowd
your disillusioned head
until the longing to be so dead
as not to feel, was tempered.
Earth bled you a little;
it was enough.

Let These Be Your Desires – Khalil Gibran

Love has no other desire but to fulfill itself
But if your love and must needs have desires,
Let these be your desires:

To melt and be like a running brook
That sings its melody to the night.
To know the pain of too much tenderness.
To be wounded by your own understanding of love;
And to bleed willingly and joyfully.
To wake at dawn with a winged heart
And give thanks for another day of loving;
To rest at the noon hour and meditate love's ecstasy;
To return home at eventide with gratitude;
And then to sleep with a prayer
For the beloved in your heart
And a song of praise upon your lips

After The Bones – Eileen Carney Hulme

Yesterday-
I thought you were
tired lost blind
to the light that fluttered
through cotton curtains
troubled by silent faces
passing in and out of
your landscape the darkness
of rivers and burning of hearts

Today-
I think you are
waiting beyond sea-lines
beyond wind-drifts reaching
into the sky multiplying stars
meditating with the moon
nothing frantic about your words
they are low soft whispers
graceful as bird song sacred at dawn.

The Artist in India – Robert Leach

Bright against obscure,
Clear against dim,
The artist lays on
Layers of paint
Carefully. Carefully
She crafts the picture –
Interior and exterior,
There and here –
While invisible in a bush
The brain fever bird:
'H-*hi-o, h-hi-o, h-hi-o, h-hi-o.*'

A local pundit
Eyes the work. 'No,'
He pronounces, and points to the dark,
The obscure. 'That colour
Is wrong, that colour
Does not exist
In India.' The artist
Does not argue
And the brain fever bird
Stays invisible in his bush:
'H-*hi-o, h-hi-o, h-hi-o, h-hi-o.*'

Hope – Anjana Basu

I called a friend and said
Tell me what hope is
He replied
"Hope is a farmer
Looking up at the thunder blue sky
With the withered earth around him
Crying in the silence"

I said to a chair
Tell me what hope is
And it replied
"Hope is a woman tied to a clock
Watching the time burn
Second by second
Closer to her flesh
Knowing her lover will come"

I asked a dog
What is hope
And he said
"Hope is following
A pair of legs and a smell
Across burning sand and molten rock
Into the mouth of the river"

I said to a tree
What is hope
And the leaves sighed
That hope was the sun's golden noose
Sent down
To pull you up into the clouds
Far far away
While the birds prayed

141

Don't Say I Said – Sophie Hannah

Next time you speak to you-know-who
I've got a message for him.
Tell him that I have lost a stone
Since the last time I saw him.
Tell him that I've got three new books
Coming out soon, but play it
Cool, make it sound spontaneous.
Don't say I said to say it.

He might ask if I've mentioned him.
Say I have once, in passing.
Memorise everything he says
And, no, it won't be grassing
When you repeat his words to me –
It's the only way to play it.
Tell him I'm toned and tanned and fine.
Don't say I said to say it.

Say that serenity and grace
Have taken root inside me.
My top-note is frivolity
But beneath, dark passions guide me.
Tell him I'm radiant and replete
And add that every day it
Seems I am harder to resist.
Don't say I said to say it.

Tell him that all my ancient faults
Have been eradicated.
I do not carp or analyse
As I might have when we dated.
Say I'm not bossy any more
Or, better still, convey it
Subtly, but get the point across.
Don't say I said to say it.

From *Pessimism For Beginners* - Carcanet, 2007

Here – Leanne McIntosh

Trust the *yes* you answer
when you are asked if you can carry
one more straw.

Trust *yes* when you spend
the currency you've kept inside
a locked chest.

Trust *yes* when you plant a seed.
Trust the hidden life
in the stone when a peach falls
over-ripe from the tree

and offer *yes* when you

are at the point of no return.
Let that be the place
you kneel to build an altar.

Dedicated to my husband, Don, who died of prostate cancer and to my son, Patrick,
who survived melanoma.

Haiku – Claire Knight

chemo over
the pink water lily you gave me
begins to open

spring sunshine
catching your fine regrowth -
watering maiden hair ferns

The Instinct Of Hope – John Clare

Is there another world for this frail dust
To warm with life and be itself again?
Something about me daily speaks there must,
And why should instinct nourish hopes in vain?
'Tis nature's prophesy that such will be,
And everything seems struggling to explain
The close sealed volume of its mystery.
Time wandering onward keeps its usual pace
As seeming anxious of eternity,
To meet that calm and find a resting place.
E'en the small violet feels a future power
And waits each year renewing blooms to bring,
And surely man is no inferior flower
To die unworthy of a second spring?

The New World – Katrina Naomi

I live in Ana's caravan,
strew it with poppies and moss.
She adds cornflowers, cow parsley,
liking colour, greens and blues.
I position the van towards the moon.

She'll sleep here
or in the woods.
I can never be sure,
but if it's a night when she's playing
with wolves, I undo the latch

and sew. I cover her bed
in Kente cloth and matted grass,
find a pink Formica table
from a seaside café that's selling up,
place it by the window,

so she can paint the stars
by numbers. I leave her
offerings of a bamboo bar,
a solar-powered record player,
scratched jazz.

I love to watch her dance,
how quetzals lift her step,
lizards pull her to the ground.
I cook a dish of cacti,

leave it steaming at her feet.

From *The Girl with the Cactus Handshake* - Katrina Naomi, Templar Poetry, 2009

147

The Lost Tribe – Anthony Rudolf
(a poem which came to me in a dream)

We are the little people,
Patient in our anonymity.

for James Hogan who dreamed up the title

Nada : hope or nothing – Richard Berengarten

Like a windblown seed, not yet rooted
or petal from an impossible moonflower, shimmering,
unplucked, perfect, in a clear night sky,

like a rainbow without rain, like the invisible
hand of a god stretching out of nowhere
to shower joy brimful from Plenty's horn,

like a greeting from a child, unborn, unconceived,
like an angel, bearing a gift, a ring, a promise,
like a visitation from a twice redeemed soul,

like a silent song sung by the ghost of nobody
to an unknown, sweet and melodious instrument
buried ages in the deepest cave of being,

like a word only half heard, half remembered,
not yet fully learned, from a stranger's language,
the sad heart longs for, to unlock its deepest cells,

a blue butterfly takes my hand and writes
in invisible ink across its page of air
Nada, Elpidha, Nadezhda, Esperanza, Hoffnung.

From *The Blue Butterfly* – Salt Publishing 2008

Intimations of Mortality – Ami Kaye

A shudder in the wind
forces me to my knees,
and I stretch inside my delicate skin.

Silence shatters and
resounds like broken glass—
perhaps the skies can endure
such loss, but can I?

Light hovers, undecided,
in diminishing strength,
but as you grow accustomed to the dark,
much that was hidden becomes visible,
the hint of impermanence brings with it
the agony, the passion to live.

Forever can be too short, and one minute enough,
if only we could learn to live in that moment,
not waiting, passive, to slide over
the edge of tomorrow.

If you must, tear open the sky, find the sun
and breathe in life . . . infuse each vein,
even if it be for a short burst of time.

Sing, my friend, exult,
soar beyond where angels gather
to scatter feathers from their broken wings.

Tears mingle with rain to nourish earth
in clear voice, pure fountain of the soul,
framed in pulsing silhouette
as songs bleed into the hungry air.

Where do souls flee when death
absorbs their radiance?
When time shrinks on itself
blooming like a treacherous flower,
so innocently cruel?

Sometimes the fallen enter memories
of those who live on wings,
like when you visit me, and my dreams,
which you inhabit fully.

Driving To Connemara – Anne Lewis-Smith

Because I love you
I have talked
(was it aloud?)
to you all morning
as I drove to Galway.
Have shared the first
sight of Arran's cliffs,
cut short the thought
of where we'd sleep
— and because I am here,
and you are there,
I do not even wonder
if you feel the same.
For I shall love you
all the way to Connemara
and the odds are
all the way back.

From *A Place Apart* – Indigo Dreams Publishing 2010

Walking With George – Ann Pilling

With George all 'puggles' are approached
with reverent slowness and the feet applied
perfectly flat for biggest splash. It seems
a dirty gum-stuck pavement is preferred
to whorling Yorkshire slabs steam-cleaned to honey
by men in orange hats. With chewing gum
his shoes can measure their bionic powers
and he his own self may decide which blob's
America, and which the sea. In Bedford Gardens
a hot sky sizzles cobalt-blue, roped thick
with creamest blossom, garlanding the street
like bunting. Small birds strafe the avenue
with twigs and pelt the ear with song. His small
egg-speckled nose lifts high, sniffing the air. This white
could be anything: snow, icing, last night's duvet
pulled over our heads to make a dragon's cave.
His hand in mine is flower-soft, he leads me
with shining face tip-tilted to the bright
enormous sky down paths I never knew
before this day, or thought I had forgotten.

From *Home Field* – Arrowhead Press

The Sphinx and the Harpy – Alan Morrison

i.m. John and Lily

I got to know my grandparents' ghosts
through crematorium recollections,
old recordings: John's tobaccoy tones
snagging on mouldy tapes, Lily's
crockery hands stacking kitchen plates...

I pictured her scrubbing stone floors at Rock,
dishcloth suffragette to chores' chained railings
...groomed by a charitable father who'd dine
alone, throwing scraps to the poor— she took
his socialisms with a spiritual tonic
of Baptist altruisms; tripe for colic;
a plaster Keir Hardie lit her heart's rose grotto
under *sui oblitus commodi*: the sphinxed
Asgills' motto: *Regardless of his own interest.*

Our country right or wrong smoked from
the khaki tongue of her patriotic husband,
unsaddled Hussar of an armchair's Northumberland...

...*she* soldiered under a Damocles of nerves
jolted by doodlebugs—but no outbursts;
just cobwebs obsessing the nooks of her thoughts;
harassments of mirrors missing out her nose;
saw herself leaping off shelf-edges
in miniature suicides...
                              ...but nothing so
tropical for her end: *cancer* —prosaic
macro-noun: nester in cells scoured to
cradle its uncancellable shadow...

...*that* harpy had ambushed John in its fast-
advancing pincer — more than a match

for all the snatching Madsens at Paschendale
that couldn't catch him: humiliations
of the guts' artilleries: stools like silkworms,
albino grubs; piss black as Lapsang Souchong...

...for Lily—teetotal, only occasional
smoker for months of a Twenties' bloom —
the mustardy crawl across her lungs was
an ill-starred scarring of abstinent tissue
for lotteries of nostalgic tar...

...a trapped doe, shivered by delirium,
she mistook my father for the ghost of her own
as he broached her dank ammonia-tomb,
betraying no tears in his elliptic eyes...

...she cradled her youngest grandson in twig-
-arms, hushabied under thundering breath
decibel by decibel distancing
its pitch from the living, till silent on
the other side of the room's partition...

Like Persephone – Patrick B Osada

You have endured.
Stolen from the light
You faced your darkness;
Bravely you returned,
With wisdom and insight.

But darkness recurred,
Gripping you softly.

Reaching out and out
It spreads across the void -
To touch all of those
You have ever loved.

(For Martina)

Palindrome – Susan Jane Sims

I have just made an egg sandwich with soft white bread,
sliced the egg with the orange plastic egg slicer
I found in Mum's drawer. And I'm back there,
the seventh of the seventh, seventy seven.
That's a palindrome the doctor said
when he called that morning to check on Mum
post cancer treatment. Later when the nausea settled
I had made her a sandwich much like this one,
the egg slightly warm. Noticed that the Christmas cacti
was blooming out of season.

Sick – Shel Silverstein

"I cannot go to school today,"
Said little Peggy Ann McKay.
"I have the measles and the mumps,
A gash, a rash and purple bumps.
My mouth is wet, my throat is dry,
I'm going blind in my right eye.
My tonsils are as big as rocks,
I've counted sixteen chicken pox
And there's one more--that's seventeen,
And don't you think my face looks green?
My leg is cut--my eyes are blue--
It might be instamatic flu.
I cough and sneeze and gasp and choke,
I'm sure that my left leg is broke--
My hip hurts when I move my chin,
My belly button's caving in,
My back is wrenched, my ankle's sprained,
My 'pendix pains each time it rains.
My nose is cold, my toes are numb.
I have a sliver in my thumb.
My neck is stiff, my voice is weak,
I hardly whisper when I speak.
My tongue is filling up my mouth,
I think my hair is falling out.
My elbow's bent, my spine ain't straight,
My temperature is one-o-eight.
My brain is shrunk, I cannot hear,
There is a hole inside my ear.
I have a hangnail, and my heart is--what?
What's that? What's that you say?
You say today is. . .Saturday?
G'bye, I'm going out to play!"

Hope – Christine Bousfield

It's the opposite of dead air,
cracking thin dark chocolate
between your teeth, discovering
a berry there; it's the feathery skin of a baby's
neck, a secret voice, rising out of nowhere,
breaking up into glittering tones, giddy rhythms.
It's lemons and butter slowly simmered over boiling water,
apples and cinnamon, new laid eggs, bacon first thing.
And this sudden word on a stone as I walk across the moor,
as if carved into the rose-indigo lines of the sky.

From *She Looks Out Of My Face* – Indigo Dreams Publishing 2011

Rooted – Minal Sarosh

While recuperating,
I felt rooted like a tree.
No! I haven't turned into one.
But, it seems I too need the sun,
to calcify my bones into fossils.

My hands are not branching out.
But, still, I drain the sea
from the glass of water.
Waves rise and my breath surfs.

The whirling fan overhead
rakes up a storm in the silence,
wants me to shed my yellow leaves
for new ones to shoot out.

My ill body digs into the mattress,
trying to reach the soil
clinging to the roots of the tree
long dead in this wooden bed.

I still say, I'm not a tree,
but have to wait like one,
for the earth, water, air and sun
to come together in me.

Nature is a stingy, thrifty housekeeper,
remixing, recycling everything
stacked in her refrigerator
and she wastes nothing in me.

But, still, unlike the tree,
there's something in me
which cannot remain rooted,
which floats freely like the clouds.

And the cawing of the crow
on the window sill, tells me
my thoughts have escaped
on its black wings.

A Way To Sing – Neil Richards

When time is short
I will show you
How days divide
Into moments
That each moment
By being lived
Has its wonder
In each wonder
A way to sing

Flame – Jodie Ford

It was hard to see the end at the beginning
sad memories to share
keeping them to ourselves

Banners to show our different offerings
all working as a team

We were connected in our thinkings
no one spoke a word

Walking through the pain
with laughter and hope
to find a cure

The road is long
we are starting to
see the light

The biggest group are
the survivors

Determination is what
strives them to fight

We need to keep this love burning
so we are closer t o what
we want to achieve

Everlasting flame
into the night

Written after taking part in the Relay For Life 2010

The No-Longer Dead – Jackie Kay

The people who are no longer dead,
who were so cold in their skin, so unlike their old selves,
have returned to the living rooms and kitchens
fields and gardens, beaches and benches,
streets, bus stops, cafes; all their favoured places.

How surprising it is, when you go to cut the hedge
or cut back the cherry blossom tree, or water the clematis,
or retile the roof, or buy from the deli some strong cheese -
how strange and pleased you are to find them coming too,
no longer gaunt; nothing left of that old disease.

Back, the long-ago-deceased, they've put weight on,
and are hanging around the old haunts,
having their open-ended conversation. You can even hear a laugh.
The voice you thought you had forgotten
has returned, with almost the same intonation.

Dear friends, you find yourself saying, *over the moon*!

Soundings – Mary MacRae

When the sensor moved cross her skin
She saw the baby hold his hands over his face

As if he were distressed. Two inches long,
His back towards us, head, body, limbs

And beating heart: how sharp it is,
This fuzzy image. He has no words, no hopes

Or thought, only instinct and shallow memories
Like those that bewilder an animal.

And passages can open out of time:
I wake one day in the dark hearing birdsong, step

From the house to the earthy smell of Spring
And plunge in, long spine, breath easy,

Like swimming with free strokes, balanced and held,
With all the blackbirds that ever were, singing.

From *Inside the Brightness of Red* - Second Light Publications 2010

Turnaround – Claire Knight

As the shock waves ebb away
an aftermath lingers   of, oh so many questions:
unfamiliar, unspeakable words have become
everyday vocabulary now.

It is part of our daily lives, part of your existence
secreted within as you went about your days –
shopping, school runs   for how long?
was it there as you watched your young son's
nativity play? or heard your daughter
speak her first words?

We speak of 'battles' and 'fighting the disease'
such harsh thoughts   and I wonder....
There is nothing foreign that invades us,
it is our own cells gone hay-wire,
run amok   what if instead we sent 'love'
and 'tenderness' to these rogue cells?
What if, in our human fragility, we befriended our
ever-present, ever-waiting soul and together swam
the waters of creation?

Is this what it would take to turn it around
and nourish ourselves
back to health?

It sparks – Claire Dyer

It is tiny, and it sparks, murmurs me
into believing that sunlight
will make cathedrals in the bracken;
there will be cheese on toast
after Sauvignon Blanc, and grey-green skies,
and Wimbledon, and the weight of you
in me, skin-to-skin; and my sons will be
the men they should become, and sheets
will applaud as they dry on the line,
and there will always be the sideways dance
of crabs, an unfolded September morning,
books, music, laughter, rain,
and long, long shadows in the dusk,
and the *News at Ten* and lavender and heat.
It is tiny, and it sparks.

Haiku – Arlene Elizabeth McGinness

Cold winter wind blows;
A seed catches the breeze and
begins a new life.

Neglected wall crumbles;
Through broken bricks a tiny plant
stretches and thrives.

Mary's Poem – Derek G A Llewellyn

You walked upon this earthly shore
But now your footsteps walk no more,
You left without me by your side
Without a kiss to say goodbye.

You were my guiding star through life,
You turned my darkness into light,
You were my inspiration too
But life has no meaning without you.

We cannot touch, we cannot see
But I know that you are here with me,
You're in my heart, you're in my mind,
Those loving thoughts forever bind.

And in the twilight of the day,
When evening shadows fade away,
I'll sit and dream of love we shared,
Those magic moments undeclared.

In loving memory of Mary Anne Llewellyn

Your Time – Geoff Stevens

Time is not linear
despite how man would have it
there are no minutes or hours in nature.
Time is forever
but it is also now; is a place.
Is where you are.
And in some places nothing happens
for days
whilst in others things change rapidly.
Time is both those places.
Time is elastic.
You can put all you want into it
all the memories of the past
the doings of now
the thoughts of the future
you can fill it with happiness
or sadness.
It would be a shame to leave it empty.
The sun can shine
the clock tick
a friend speak
you smile
the cat miaow
a tear run down the cheek
all at the same moment.
Time is with you
place it on your knee
and stuff it with thoughts.
Time is not going anywhere
no matter what those horologists say.
They don't own it
no clockmaker can take yours away.
It's with you always.
Grasp it closely

fill it full of hope
tell it what to do
and if it's getting ahead of itself
call it back
tell it to hold on a bit
you haven't finished with it yet.

Story Line – Ginny Sullivan

While you lie
linked
to the sleek streamlining of chrome
and plastic
as delicate as the tendrils
of deep-sea creatures
in a reversal of the umbilicus
that once fed and formed you,
now stripping you by taking away,
now depleting you by casting
napalm through your body,
you wait hand-held
for the mercurial currents
to wash your cells,
for this strange fluid
to strip and scour
the oceanic depths of you,
and your blood
is lost in the dilution of water
faded and petal-edged as it
disappears into the colourlessness
of its surroundings
until
you
lie levitated and stripped to your core

and this core
is
still and small,
is
all movement and all space,
is
as luminous as white cotton blown sunwards,
as flint and light-struck as diamond and pearl.

Being there,
you allow what is happening,
have what upholds you,
let the words of your grandchildren
fill you with joy
that seeps into the spaces
left by the filtering
the draining
the clearing
so that your veins flow with love
and your heart is rendered
by the sanctity of these new pathways.

A Sawdust Day – Dawn Bauling

It is a sawdust day
when the edges of life
lie at my feet, useless,
roughly chipped and grated,
ready to be blown by others'
footsteps in the wind.

It is a sawdust day
when words lose their taste
and I can't concentrate
on anything but husks,
desperately seeking spice
but finding only rice.

It is a sawdust day
when possibility pops
before I can catch it
or stop it lap dancing
provocatively out of reach,
teasing me with rainbows.

But I will not be choked
and can hope for more than
raw skin and tasteless crusts
as the carpenter works.
For he will send me chilli
flowers to scatter in the dust.

From *Loud Voices in the Quiet Child* – Indigo Dreams Publishing 2008

We People Too – Benjamin Zephaniah

I have dreams of summer days
Of running freely on the lawn
I luv a lazy Sunday morn
Like many others do.
I luv my family always
I luv clear water in a stream
Oh yes I cry and yes I dream
We dogs are people too.

And I dear folk am small and great
My friends call me the mighty Bruce
I luv to drink pure orange juice
Like many others do.
I hope you all appreciate
We give you all a helping hand
When me and my friends turn the land
We worms are people too.

When I have time I luv sightseeing
You may not want to see my face
But you and me must share a space
Like many others do.
Please think of me dear human being
It seems that I'm always in need
I have a family to feed
We mice are people too.

They say we're really dangerous
But we too like to feel and touch
And we like music very much
Like many others do.
Most of us are not poisonous
I have a little lovely face
I move around with style and grace
We snakes are people too.

I don't mind if you stand and stare
But know that I have luv no end
And my young ones I will defend
Like many others do.
When you see me in the air
Remember that I know the worth
Of all us who share the earth
We birds are people too.

I need fresh air and exercise
I need to safely cross the road,
I carry such a heavy load
Like many others do.
Don't only judge me by my size
Ask any veterinarian
I'm just a vegetarian
We cows are people too.

Water runs straight off my smooth back
And I hold my head high with pride
I like my children at my side
Like many others do.
I don't care if you're white or black
If you like land or air or sea
I want to see more unity
We ducks are people too.

I think living is so cool
And what I really like the most
Is kiss chase and I luv brown toast
Like many others do.
I hang around in a big skool
I only need a little sleep
I like thinking really deep
We fish are people too.

I luv the cows I love the trees
And I would rather you not smoke
For if you smoke then I would choke
Like many others do.
I beg you do not squash me please
I do not want to cause you harm
I simply want you to stay calm
We flies are people too.

My name is Thomas Tippy Tops
Billy is not my name
I've learnt to live with fame
Like many others do.
I once was on Top of the Pops
On TV I sang loud
My parents were so proud
We goats are people too.

I luv to walk among the fern
I'm thankful for each night and day
I really luv to holiday
Like many others do.
I've read the books and my concern
Is why do we always look bad
My friends don't think I'm raving mad
We wolves are people too.

A lovely garden makes me smile
A good joke makes me croak
One day I want to own a boat
Like many others do.
I'd luv to see the river Nile
I'd luv my own sandcastle
I really want to travel
We frogs are people too.

Please do not call me horrid names
Think of me as a brother
I'm quite nice you'll discover
Like many others do.
If you're my friend then call me James
I'll be your friend forever more
I'll be the one that you adore
We pigs are people too.

We really need this planet
And we want you to be aware
We just don't have one spare
Not any of us do.

We dogs, we goats
We mice, we snakes
Even we worms
Are really great,
We birds, we cows
We ducks, we frogs
Are just trying to do our jobs
We wolves, we fish
We pigs, we flies
Could really open up your eyes
And all we want to say to you
Is that
We all are people too.

From *Too Black, Too Strong* - Bloodaxe Books, 2001

Hymn to Mastectomy – Chrys Salt

Here's to the woman with one tit
who strips down to her puckered scars
and fronts the mirror – doesn't give a shit
for the pert double breasted wonderbras
sneaking a furtive gander
at her missing bit.

'Poor lady,' they are thinking
'can her husband bear to touch her?
Will she ever dare to wear
that slinky low-cut sweater'?

Here's to the woman with half a bust
who wears her lack of symmetry
with grace and moist with lust
offers a single nipple like a berry
to her lover's tongue.
Here's to the single breasted ones
come home victorious from the wars,
wearing their wounds
as badges on the chests
of Amazons.

'She ought to cover up
it's embarrassing, it's shocking.
I'm sure she thinks she's very brave
but <u>everybody's</u> looking'!

Here's to those wondrous affrontages
out on the scene in sauna, pool and gym,
those who when whole were dying –
now less than whole
become themselves again.

Hands – Heidi Williamson

You haven't told me
why your hands are clenching
in time with your mother's breathing.

But I know you are urging
each breath on, counting
them in with minute stresses,

and you are shielding
us both from your hope
in this small engine of love.

Trees -- X   rays
of   hands – Ewa Chrusciel

Your mother gave you a ginkgo leaf before she died:
a thousand-year-old inhabitant of the Permian oceans grows
inside us. We understand well cambium cells of waiting.
We began with evanescence and now we think of each other
in terms of light. Do you see a mustard seed in a mulberry tree?
We would like only for once to get where we are already.
My mother, too, is an entrapped ghost, her venous mesh of neurons
colliding in cacophonies, her head full of yellow secrets.
Their leaves push me forward. I walk the Manhattan streets to meet her,
I kneel and pick more Ginkgo leaves and wield them like oars.
51 cranes scraping the sky with the geometry of crosses. Before I leave,
my mother stops in a park and collects—the groves inside us.

Dust – Alison Lock

I open the flower press
release the dust remains.
Anemones. Their stalks
once refracted in a glass bowl,
petals of red, indigo,
creamy white, centres black.

Behind the curtain Nana lay dying
and I thought she'd slipped
into morphinous sleep, so I too
slipped out. Later, on the table
were the fallen petals
and a vase full of tears.

To my dear Nana, who loved anemones

From *A Slither of Air* – Indigo Dreams Publishing 2011

Light Soul – Luis Rivas Takeda

Hope is the softest kiss to the air
and the solid substance of tears.

The breath of hope
like the wind blows,
and carries shapes of life,
contained in the vapour
of exhaled wishes.

Clouds of hope stream
in the river of the air,
floating along
an unfathomable destiny.
Precipitating life, like the gift of water,
to the driest desert,
to the neediest soul,
to the hottest spirit.

Hope is a light at the centre of the universe,
where life begins, in its cyclic eternity.

Light travels immeasurable distances,
sometimes from the eyes to the heart.

Letting Go – Valerie Morton

There is a silence in the room;
a moment when the candle flickers
and in the centre of the flame
I see the shape of you, fingertips
stretching towards me.

I know if we touch there will be pain,
pain. I've left a light in many cathedrals
across the world. But now, as night
gives way to a different day
I close my eyes and there you go,

shooting into the sky –
a rocket: gold, red and blue.

Fragile Feathers – Stephanie MacDonald

Their voices can be heard
floating on the lightest breeze,
quiet as the mourning dove
sighing at the waking dawn.

These shining guardians unseen,
wander to our melancholy souls;
whispering assurances of protection
when all hope begins to wane.

Silently they grace us with
tender hands upon our shoulders.
Gently pushing in our hesitations,
leading us from the depths of obscurity.
Lifting us… dusting us…
if we should stumble along our path.

In the most tentative of times,
they will glide along beside us,
to light our way through darkened hours
when we are troubled most.

They embrace us in their radiance;
warming our spirits and our minds.
No trace of their existence, bar
fragile feathers drifting in their wake.

This – Osip Mandelstam

This is what I most want
unpursued, alone
to reach beyond the light
that I am furthest from.

And for you to shine there-
no other happiness-
and learn, from starlight,
what its fire might suggest.

A star burns as a star,
light becomes light,
because our murmuring
strengthens us, and warms the night.

And I want to say to you
my little one, whispering,
I can only lift you towards the light
by means of this babbling.

Tears Of Hope – Josie Lawson

As a child I didn't know what cancer meant. As I grew, it was in the news. I knew it was bad, people kept dying. Chemotherapy was mentioned. It hit home one day when a friend sought my ear. She had been diagnosed with breast cancer and I felt tears inside my soul. She was given the all clear.

A few years down the line a great friend of mine developed it too. She had two young children. She was my writer friend and one day, the police came round when I was visiting. Someone had sabotaged her car on the way to chemo. As time went on, I found out one day my friend had died in peace in a hospice. My tears cried towards heaven.

Hope is a many outlandish thing. People research and cancer organisations help. Sometimes they come up with an answer -

HOPE, that is the true word. My aunt, she was in remission a lot...

My mother developed bowel cancer...she got over it

But she died a few years later...

My aunt, mums sister, became a second mum to me, but one day, my tears became a like an ocean: My aunt died....of cancer, she could not hold on any more. And so, as I remember, I remember also the times in front of us, the hope for the rest of us...Kylie Minogue she survived; Jade, she died. But many, many now live to tell the tale.

Me, well, my pituitary tumour was not cancer, It was benign...but I am being monitored as it could grow again. So let our world, our people, our volunteers aid the future - *hope* is the theme....

Dedication
I hope these words will be of use to all who read. I am glad research is always being done, giving hope for all others in our land who may be hit with some form of cancer, and I thank the editors and Macmillan nurses who support for inviting me to write for this anthology which will hopefully increase their funds so that they will be able to support many more...

Seahorses – Hazel Frew

Hopes are
seahorses,
elegant urchin.

Bubbles in glasses
treble clefs.

There's a spring
of them bursting
Ka-pow-ing daily.

Despite the
furrows
in my face.

Wear the Treasure of the Day – David Seddon

When melancholy morning weaves
A mouldered coat of sorry sheaves
We wreathe the future in despair
And breathe the past in present air.

So smelt the mulling midnight's lead
And forge the present's golden thread
Then wear the treasure of the day
With past and future flung away!

'In Silk and Steel..' – Sullivan the Poet

In silk and steel, their darkest arts,
Stoop surgeons all to weave;
Their pagan spells in blood and flesh,
Upon this fragile bloom:
While yet this tender, gentle form,
No moment's soft reprieve;
Or let its torment's daily yoke,
To light the deathly gloom.

No god give day, no morn, no hour,
Lies placid with its kin;
No docile night passed free the stings,
Those sharp and silken bites:
Nor solace brings the gut churned day,
For 'neath that pallid skin;
All drip, drip, drip, a devil's brew,
Cruel every cell ignites!

Oh! Frail and sickly, feeble child,
So small a life to spare;
Each trembling beat but bare a pulse,
All breath a titan's trial:
No lock or curl to drape your brow,
Nor lash to shade day's glare;
But torments set to test the saints,
To spiteful gods revile.

And yet; within that fragile shell,
So feeble, fraught and small;
There beats a heart, though troubled sore,
That will no quarter give:
An iron will in velvet guise,
As hard as granite spall;
That will not cede one paltry inch,
Within its fight to live.

A warrior soul in tender flesh,
Ribbed through in brightest steel;
No easy meat the Reaper's blade,
Nor yet so meek or mild:
This battle joined lays far from lost,
No hand upon this deal;
Oh fearful shade, seek prey elsewhere ,
You shall not have *this* child!

Visitation - Maitreyabandhu

Strange that you should come
like that, without any form at all,
carrying no symbolic implements,
without smile or frown
or any commotion,
as if you had been there all the time,
like a pair of gloves left in a pocket.

As if I had been looking *that* way,
into the wide blue yonder, and you were
beside me, enduring my hard luck stories
with infinite patience. Not even waiting –
the tree outside my window
doesn't wait, nor the ocean-wedge
with its new, precise horizon – just *there*
like the shadow of a church

or a quiet brother.
And how I saw you, in the mess of things,
was as a slant of grey,
the perfect grey of house dust,
an absolute neutral, with no weaving,
no shimmer of cobalt
and light-years away from Byzantium.

Grey. And I want to add, like light,
as if a skylight opened in my skull,
and into the darkness fell
a diagonal of pure Bodmin Moor.
But even that's too bright,
too world-we're-busy-in.
Call it 'dust' then, or the bloom
of leaf-smoke from an autumn fire.

Winner of the Manchester Cathedral Religious Poetry Prize in 2007 and the Geoffrey Dearmer Prize in 2009

For Kevin, My Macmillan Nurse – Gill McEvoy

You didn't laugh at my protesting
that I wasn't seriously ill,
nor at my boasts that I would beat this thing,
and once again be well.

You never disagreed with anything
I told you I'd achieve
(things that would have always been beyond
all possibility).

Instead you got me morphine
for the pain,
medicine for the raging inflammation
in my bones and veins.

When I think of the outrageous things I said,
I feel ashamed,
recall the way you said I was *remarkable*,
how I believed it then.

But I was just a person desperately afraid -
and *that* you knew.
You held out sympathetic hands; in them lay
the tiny egg of blue

called hope. For me it opened, spread out wings
and flew.
I know now that the one *remarkable*
was you.

Like A Bird – Susan E Smith

Sometimes I forget her
In the dark, stark hours
Before dawn.
She's locked out
And stays rejected,
Seemingly forever.
I pale, forlorn and waiting;
Alone.
As the sun rises, she comes
Tapping at the window,
Feathers dashed against the panes.

I let her inside.
She's unhurt, intact; perfect.
In the morning
She comes home
And stays, cherished,
Seemingly forever.
During daylight, forborne and patient;
Constant.
As the sun sets, I open up,
Holding on to her
Feathers bristling in my hands

I clasp her gently,
Her wings under my fingers.
A heartbeat's throbbing, between
Careful palms,
Inside a breast
Made of voile-like bone
And paper-thin skin.
She is a fragile thing;
Her breath's imperceptable
In the silence.

I hold her in my heart,
Her light flowing through my skin;
A glow, glimmering and glittering,
From within.
Outside, a smile
As resilient as stone,
Flexing not bowing.
She is the strongest thing;
Her power's impeachable
In the radiance

Our strength grows, together again;
She won't leave me now.
I've taken her in
And taken her on.
She brings me brightness in the dark;
She is my solitary shadow.
She is birdsong in sleep;
A whisper becomes a roar.
In my dreams, a consort;
She alone helps me soar.

She Explained – Michael James Treacy

She was distracted
and he ran on the pitch
in an instinctive,
uninhibited,
exhilarating chase
along the right wing.

He out-stripped
the startled player,
gave the ball
an almighty kick
and followed up
with a round of applause
as he watched it
cannon off the post
and career into the stands.

She explained
that he always clapped
when he was proud
of something he'd achieved,
so they all laughed
and agreed it was an excellent kick,
most of them applauded
and someone shouted,
"Well done, that man!"

He suffered
her gentle admonishment
when he returned
dutifully to her side
and the match
attained normality
as he retreated
back to his world,
with his secret smile
perceptibly wider.

Moonrise – Naomi Foyle

i.m. Brenda Macdonald Riches

Witwalking. Her favourite way
of writing. Leave a sentence half-finished,
so you always know where to begin. The sentence
is a nubby twig about to split, a maze of new directions,
splintering underfoot. The last word is her forefinger, pointing,
not at me, but up, always up, to that vast realm where beauty, bliss
and genius dwell when not at home. Or did she only do that once,
lean forward out of her Lazy Boy recliner, index finger alerting me to
...what? A passage of Beethoven, Katherine Mansfield, Wallace Stevens?
Or a full moon I've forgotten, for unlike her fingers, thinner than mine,
oval-tipped, the moon still nightly sets its changing prints against the sky.
She's climbed beyond me now, but that half-buried latticework she kicked
down into my brain mulch still crackles in her wake — her in the basement,
drinking Brown Cows, instructing me about Edie Sedwick's tits: *if they stick up*
when she's flat on her back, they're fake. Or laughing at her second favourite joke,
unspellable: *How does a woman hold her liqueur?* Answer: *by the ears.* That was
my sex education, along with two books on teenage anatomy, blue for boys,
scarlet for girls, left in a drawer with a box of condoms and a note: *Don't*
tell Dad. Did she tell me how to figure out your porn star billing? Mother's
maiden name, and the name of your first pet: I'd be Polly Papodopolous.
Buttons bursting through the ceiling, with bare hands and blinding teeth,
Polly shrinks the Child Catcher, gathers all the stolen boys and girls like
flowers to her breasts. Her bristle-chinned Mama, weeping with pride,
waves a crooked finger, puts a witwalker's spell on my soul. Coz it's
sure as hell been a ziggety-zag-jagged trip-hop-trap crunch-time-pop
kinda life, and here I am now, forty years old, peeing blue ink
in the dust by the side of the road, in love with the sun
on my cunt, shimmying into the simmering night,
saying *yes* to it all: looking back, looking up,
writing home in a soft future light

The Damaged Tree – Denise Bennett

Here I find the damaged tree
which leans to the light sideways,
a nap of moss where the hurt-side
has healed.

Not showy like the rhododendron
where wind whiffles scarlet skirts,
nor prissy like the white frothy
myrtle in full flower.

Something of my stoical self
hides here in twisted limbs;
I touch the mended flesh
a miracle of sun and wind has fused.

Another box of nipples arrived today – Char March

The hospital computer's gone mad
– that's the third box this week.
You stick them on the fridge door,
the phone, the handle of the kettle.
And we laugh. Then you are sick again.

This evening you sit in your usual chair
in the bloat of chemo, your breath really
bothering you. And me, if truth be told.
You are darning pullovers neither of us
ever wear – and even Oxfam won't take.

What if I could give you a new pair?
That will always pass the pencil test, even
at 90; with dark aureoles and pert
tips that tilt cheekily, but don't
show through your tennis dress.

You are muttering about camels
and licking the thread for the *n*th time;
specs half-way down – in your usual chair.
I don't see hacked-at womanhood,
that you've sobbed salt-herring barrels for.

I see you. Darning your way to normality.

From *The thousand natural shocks* – Indigo Dreams Publishing 2011

The Open Door – Ruth Padel

(for Nikos Stavroulakis)

What is not exile? Beginning is flight.
The end is free flow of the breath.
Rumi of Afghanistan. I am inside
your looking, I wait to be light.

Rustle of water, of wind.
Away from my own soul, cling
to the surface, hold to the depths
as tired eyes look forward to sleep.

Cold mountain. Cave-shadow. Rusty cliffs
glow in the lake. Why should I seek?
A hand closes - and opens like wings
of a bird. You are where I am.

Tremble of aquamarine. White mosque.
Radio mast silhouette on the peak.
What you thought you had lost.
Praise those who wake early, in grief.

Coming To Dartmoor – Ronnie Goodyer

Maybe you'll come when the hazel catkins
wave the promise of autumn fruit,
or heavy frost is melted by sun
turning meadow-grass to bright chandeliers.

Maybe you'll come when the bluebells and purple orchids
lead to new primroses by the wood
and hawthorn-scented air rises above the pink
of bell-heather and western gorse.

Maybe you'll come when the pearl fritillary
blows to the wild violets,
or larval clover gives birth to common blue,
opening its page-wings to green alkanet.

Maybe you'll avoid the boggy ground
where forget-me-nots thrive beside moorland streams,
yellow asphodel and St John's Wort form bright towers
and cotton-grass heads wait to fly.

Maybe you'll resist running wild with ponies,
shouting loud from granite tors,
circling with windless, weightless buzzards
and be happily unknown in the wilderness.

Maybe you'll leave in a foxglove-summer,
carrying its memory in the heart and stars,
or when heathers' perfume lies on the warm days drift
and the unicorns gather to graze......

From *Indigo Dreams Revisited* – Indigo Dreams Publishing 2010

The Flowers That I Left In The Ground – Leonard Cohen

The flowers that I left in the ground,
that I did not gather for you,
today I bring them all back,
to let them grow forever,
not in poems or marble,
but where they fell and rotted.

And the ships in their great stalls,
huge and transitory as heroes,
Ships I could not captain,
today I bring them back
to let them sail forever,
not in model or ballad,
but where they were wrecked and scuttled.

And the child on whose shoulders I stand,
whose longing I purged
with public, kingly discipline,
today I bring him back
to languish forever,
not in confession or biography,
but where he flourished,
growing sly and hairy.

It is not malice that draws me away,
draws me to renunciation, betrayal:
it is weariness, I go for weariness of thee.
Gold, ivory, flesh, love, God, blood, moon-
I have become the expert of the catalogue.

My body once so familiar with glory,
my body has become a museum:
this part remembered because of someone's mouth,
this because of a hand,
this of wetness, this of heat.

Who owns anything he has not made?
With your beauty I am as uninvolved
as with horses' manes and waterfalls.
This is my last catalogue.
I breathe the breathless
I love you, I love you—
and let you move forever.

From *The Spice Box of Earth* - Jonathan Cape. Reprinted by permission of The
Random House Group Ltd.

Vision – Mahmood Farzan

On the far horizon of thought,
I looked for a messenger to fill my vision.

A shadow passed by me whispering,
'Fill the chalice of your eyes with sleep,
So you may see the stars' dreams.'

I heard the night fall
And overwhelm the heft of day.
Dust lay on my eyes.
                              The vision darkened.

A breeze passed by me whispering,
'Bathe your eyes in moonlight,
So you may see the stars' reflection'

I heard the storm hammer.
A heavy cloud filled the sky of my eyes,
And its burden fell on my cheeks.
                              The vision clouded.

A stream passed by me whispering,
'Rub your eyes with the parched desert,
So you may feel the stars' proximity.'

I heard the deluge rolling brutally
Down the stream's path,
And its furrow scarred my face.
                              The vision shuddered.

A sigh passed by me whispering,
'Wash your eyes with salty tears,
So you may see the stars' brightness.'

I felt pain overcome my soul,
And coldness lie
On my heart and bones.

                                    The vision suffered.

A spark passed by me whispering,
'Wash your eyes with the light of truth,
So you may feel the stars' presence.'

I felt hope enter my heart
And cleanse my pulse.
Radiance filled my eyes,

                                    And the vision became love.

On the far horizon of thought,
I looked for the messenger
Who filled my vision with love.

Map Making – Jan Fortune-Wood

An edge of flag –

unfurling at the limits
of these names,

borders blend—
muffled green that slides
to grey that mutes
to biscuit-earth.

And to the west, the margin
of a ragged land
frays into a tattered sea
that will not let me
sink.

These I Have Loved – Grace Galton

The voice of Domingo, the art of Van Gogh,
the rose pink flamingo, Shakespeare and Belloc.
Circus performers from slim wires suspended
and birds flying freely as nature intended.

Love's sweet enchantment. - the first light of dawning.
the skylark exultant on a sweet summer morning.
First smile of an infant and - Reggae – Jamaican!
and lemon scent, pungent - and sizzling bacon!

The web of a spider with sky shining through,
the down of the eider - and singing bamboo.
The plopping of raindrops through canopied trees,
a gurgling stream or the sigh of a breeze.

A lop-sided scarecrow. - the portent of swallows
a beauteous rainbow and the blue sky that follows.
The laughter of children enthralled by a clown,
the first star of evening and the sun going down.

The sails of a windmill, - Buonarotti's 'Pieta'
the singing of violins and musical theatre.
The feel of your hand on my brow when I'm fevered.
The embrace on my skin as the boat turns to windward.

A smile from stranger, pure creamy white doves,
the sensuous feeling of soft doeskin gloves.
A burgeoning Spring – Summer's long carefree days,
the abundance of Autumn – horse-drawn Winter sleighs.

The Lord's gift of senses all leading me through
a world fill with beauty – sights much loved – and new.

What You Will – Julia O'Brien
(for Lily)

For now it is invisible and warm:
this blanket I have woven for you, dreamt
around you. If some day you wake and feel
constricted, take the time to look. Please look.
See silver leaves, like rabbits' ears, kiss rings
of scented jasmine; clouds of muted blues
and greens bleed cockled paths through darkling seas
reflected in myriad embroidered mirrors.
This is yours, please take it: pluck it, teasel
where it feels too smooth, too tough; gently loose
the warp from weft and rupture where it cramps
but keep whatever's left to weave another.
Your legacy may be a lighter gift,
my daughter; make of my one what you will.

Today – Ashley Bovan

in the park,
I hear an organ grinder,
Nellie the Elephant leaves the circus.

The corner shop
has 3 for 2
on chocolate milk

and from this bench,
I see the clouds drift away
for a couple hours of sun.

Hidden – Sara Boyes

And after I hid my frustration
  but wounded you
with my ever-driving turning away,

and you hid your fear and wounded me
  with your cutting put-down of my capacities -
how to make a place where a seed may grow?

How to quell
  the petty oughts and aspirations of the ego
and dig over new, fresh soil?

Seek behind the knife-like edges of broken mirror
  in the soft moist dark
and face the desperate despairs that

now, maybe, is the end of life
  when striving for rewards in the world
must be relinquished?

For it is in this soft moist dark,
  by digging deeper
and speaking

- I to you, and you to me -
  that yet we may plant a seed
and new life may grow.

For my son who came to live at home while receiving treatment.

Published in Acumen 63, Jan 2009.

Waking up together – Sabine Huynh

In the dead of night
from black to blue to white
faint bird notes fall
one by one
light nears

from his heart to her hand
thousands of kilometres
of veins capillaries in crumpled bedsheets
they've travelled years to get there

a crow caws ahead of the alarm-clock
her bloodflow the ticking
fail to merge together
until his first smile
echoes hers.

We Have – Stella Rotenberg

We have nothing
but our flesh
- and vulnerability

October – Stella Rotenberg

A rich harvest beneath a gloomy sky
and without a care around my pain
bloom roses

From: Stella Rotenberg, *SHARDS,* translated by Donal McLaughlin &
Stephen Richardson, Edinburgh 2003

New Year Snow – Frances Horovitz

For three days we waited,
a bowl of dull quartz for sky.
At night the valley dreamed of snow,
lost Christmas angels with dark-white wings
flailing the hills.
I dreamed a poem, perfect
as the first five-pointed flake,
that melted at dawn:
a Janus-time
to peer back at guttering dark days,
trajectories of the spent year.
And then snow fell.
Within an hour, a world immaculate
as January's new-hung page.
We breathe the radiant air like men new-born.
The children rush before us.
As in a dream of snow
we track through crystal fields
to the green horizon
and the sun's reflected rose.

Calm – John Kinsella

I've managed to get through today
without a major attack of anxiety:
when the eagle flew out of the gully
the shadow of its wings seemed untroubled,
and sounds in the distance were vague
and damage-free. I even discovered
a sapling I thought shrivelled
and killed off by heat, fatigue
in the roots tapped by sandalwood
forgotten as I discovered a pair
of sandalwoods I'd not known were there.
The evening is mild for this time of year
and the light joins imperfections
and different textures alike. I won't sully
the picture with anxieties I keep at bay,
and will resolve night fraction by fraction.

sanguine – Lawrence Upton

He thought it was an angel breaking out
of a fire and its snapping bright reflections,
hot glass falling in pieces; and the wind
rising, rousing harsh fear amongst many
shouting advice and trying to recall
how to pray. He thought it was a helper;
and he wanted help, now, as time ended.
What might appear evil burned towards him.
One figure glowed and disappeared into
a surf of light and flame splinters thrown up
from burning waves' damage while pushed inwards
on a tide warning vital thirsty organs.
He followed without hope, and, yet, sanguine,
that he would last if his will persisted.

Sugar – Angela Topping

A recipe sure to dry tears:
white bread, yellow butter,
sifting of sugar
folded over and taken outside
to eat in the gutter
superciliously watching the game
still going on in the echoing square.

Taunts fly off without touching
because you can say
I don't care: I've got a sugar butty.
More tangible than a mother's kiss
and brisk 'never mind', a sign,
a caress you could show off
that someone cared enough,
as you bite into the sticky grit
and feel the sugar rush.

Even now, in this grown up world
when the game goes on without you
and you're pushed into dusty gutter
there's someone
to make that cup of tea,
set everything to rights.

When Instant Coffee Just Isn't Instant Enough – Luke Wright

"Bake for 20 minutes at 200 degrees… Nuts to that, I'll cook it for one minute at 1000 degrees!" – Homer Simpson

What is it exactly you plan to do
with all the moments you saved; the short cut
through the dodgy estate, the microwave,
the dashed escalator, the Oyster Card
the long hot baths that became quick showers?

How will you hoard them? Stacked in the garage?
Stuffed inside a soiled mattress? Or perhaps
just lined up on the book case like prizes,
bottles of wine with peeled labels,
left to mature before you take your quiet sips.

Studied, deliberate, smug. And knowing that
everyone else has blown all of theirs
on three course meals, the scenic route to work,
and an extra pint on Fridays. While you
were making your chronological deals,

buying easy-iron, half-cotton shirts,
hurtling towards death without a
single second left to contemplate
a lifetime sat in cafes watching the door,
twiddling your thumbs and catching your breath.

First published in *High Performance* - Nasty Little Press (2009)

The Night It Stayed Light – Paul Goring

The night it stayed light
We closed our conversations
Ended them
Finished what we had to say
On the very same day
That we started them

There was no hour to leave
Or a time to arrive
Curtains remained un-drawn
We could see into everywhere
And it seemed that the sun hovered
Between the hills for hours

The night it stayed light
Your eyes stayed open
You never closed them
Not even a blink
I stared into them for an eternity
And meant it completely

There was no next day or today
To separate us
The cock crowed in mid-afternoon
And we drank hot chocolate
For breakfast like the French do,
We strange cosmopolitans

The night it stayed light
The owl never flew and the bats waited
Patient in barns
And I looked at you in pyjamas at noon
With sunlight on your hair
And I felt humble
For being allowed to love you
All that long day

Published with kind permission of Flarestack Publishing

Woman in the Mirror – Bernadette Davidson

How enormous her eyes,
her ears, commas against a naked face.
How elegant the curve of head,
egg shell scalp, shiny, smooth.

How her turquoise silk scarf
wrapped around her hairless head,
matched her eyes.
How the dangling silver glittered on her ears.

How she imagined herself a Buddhist nun,
a French whore after liberation,
Joan of Arc   mounted on her horse
Nefertiti without her golden crown.

How somehow she was released
from the struggle with brush and comb
Vanity now placed in the drawer
along side the curling iron and hair spray.

Northbound train – Sue Vickerman

Reading about loss, I look up
as Holy Island goes by us
on the flat palm of the sea.
The conductor clips my ticket
during a difficult paragraph,
the hard fact of a death.

A steward serves tea and biscuits
as we pass through Berwick.
The immensity, the smallness of it,
plot or scattered ashes.

Kircaldy. November closing over us,
sky turning yellow. The sea lies leaden
as we skirt Montrose's basin.
Northwards looks dark like oblivion

but an end is also a beginning:
there is talk of future happiness.

Aberdeen. A passage about lighthouses –
how their beams are never broken –
and incredibly we pass a lighthouse,
and its light seems miraculous.

Dreaming My Sister – Catherine Whittaker

I dream her alive.

Hear her singing in the house by the sea
brave as seagulls diving,
joking and cooking
in her cluttered kitchen.

Dream her alive.

Feel her arms when I cry
over some boy breaking me apart.
Hear the strong beat of her heart,
taste smoke and aniseed.

Dream her in dusk-light
spilling out words
like moths drawn to her
lavender-scented candles,

dream I remember each one.
Dream her alive,

that I have never touched
the hard, smooth, stone of despair,
felt the steel-jawed mouth
of remorse.

Dream her young,
in her orange dress, laughing,
energy blazing out,
a flare falling on water.

Dream her whispering nursery rhymes,
in wind-haunting nights,
breath soft on my face
keeping me safe.
I dream her alive.

Dedicated to my late sister

Published in *Artemis* issue 3 2009

First Light – D M Thomas

I'd whooping cough, so I was told,
life-threatening, when I was six months old;

and I recall as though it were today
what must have been a fierce cough racking me

although I seem outside my own distress
till I can breathe again. Primal, it's less

a memory than something I still feel,
as real as now is. There's a woman's pale

face looking on, upset: I'm sure, my aunt's;
and I am being held, although I can't

feel mother's arms: I seem to float
mid-air. It's murky, from my sight

being still imperfect, but I'm aware
of the pale face, and larger paleness where

I'll later know one looks out at a carn.
This is where I'm for an instant born

into myself, a being in the world,
and I don't feel the cough, nor being held,

but love I see and feel, bound up with light.
And both seem known to me, and infinite.

The Soul of Spring – Paul McDonald

One dull day in March
he pulls his woollen hat
below his ears.
All he sees is desert:
too little for a poem of one word.
No snappy clothes, no drink.
No cards, dice, or horses.
No sporting girls.
All he has is hunger
like a tramp, or a holy man.

One fine day in May
he throws his woollen hat
onto a hook.
The soul of spring thrills
him into season,
stiffens him to sugar.
Now is when it all begins,
the list of kicks:
the man who juggles knives
in an overcoat of fur;
the acrobat who swings
between two chairs. Or better.
The play performed to ringing bells;
the banjoist; the peasants
stroking gipsy folk on fiddles.

From *An Artist Goes Bananas* – Indigo Dreams Publishing 2011

Box – Neil Richards

When hope was the last thing left in the box, we opened it to see what hope was like, but all we could find at the bottom was another box. When it touched sunlight it grew to the exact shape and size of the original. We look inside this new box.

Super Birds – Donna Beck

They cheer on the sun
Treating its un-failing spread of light
As if it were new
This thrill of musical chests
Beaks of lyrical treasures
Describe to the rising
To any listening ear
How they view a miracle
A re-appearing world
Before wetting their deserving throats
On caterpillars and worms

Black Bull – Mark Roper

Winter's doing its best
to wipe him out.
One minute an ice-house,
the next he's a riverbed.

Murdered by mist,
razored raw by wind,
he's a black fact
frost doesn't credit.

Hunched in his muscle,
no look in his eye,
feet forgotten in mire,
he has to stand for it.

The great roof of his neck
sags, starts to leak.
Through his skull's tunnel
the draughts pour.

Everyone's in but him
and all he can do
is let the worst occur
and let it occur again.

By spring he's gone
though there he is,
dancing down the fence
beside the cattle,

flicking up his dainty feet,
bellowing like a boy,
thick strings of drool
dropping on new grass.

For Jim Daly, Roz Gill, Mary Herbert, Nuala Hurley, Eddie Keen, Jim Nolan, Ted and Mary O'Regan and Lewis Roper.

One Small Thing – Darren Couchman

Well that's it then, I've got the big C
It's already taken my parents and now it's got me
My dreams at night are full of sorrow and despair
Why can't I dream good things, instead of these terrible nightmares

My emotions take over, my head is all over the place
I completely lose control when I see my wife's face
What have I done to deserve such a fate
How long have I got, how long is the wait?

Then something happened, something so small
But this small something made me realise that I'd been a fool
I pictured my kids doing things without me,
Simple things like riding their bikes and having their tea

The look on their faces killed me inside
And from that moment on I knew I could fight
No more was the sorrow, gone the despair
I had to fight my cancer and make sure I was there

The cancer may have took my Mum and my Dad
But I was going nowhere and boy am I glad
My fight grew stronger as did my love for my life
And I just kept picturing my kids and my wife

I am now with my kids as they play on the swings
Such a simple pleasure, such a simple little thing
But they mean so much to me as my fight carries on
Well I haven't been beaten I am now so strong

My life is now different, I live for every day
And I have one simple message, so listen to what I say
I spent too many days crying and boy did I mope
But it only takes one small thing to give you that hope

Darren Couchman, testicular cancer survivor and author of One Lump or Two

Upholding the 'I' – Moniza Alvi

I try to uphold the 'I'
to push it upright

the clear, straight 'I'
stalking onwards

or resting on its back
the horizontal 'I'
like a log across a stream

the 'I' leaning to one side,
aslant in the afternoon sun,

the best time for photographs.

*

The naked 'I' in an unused room
tall enough to peer out of the window.

The 'I' shouts for clothes
for a cloak to trail on the lakeside turf
for padded shoulders.

The 'I' has strange proportions.

*

'We' are its cousins,
its close confederates.

The 'I' crashes around,
trying to find its own way.

But what could be called 'its own' –
the arrows it shoots in the dark?

*

The 'I' is gold dust –
a crocus in the mouth

a smear of mustard
the bellow of the sun.

*

The 'I'.

No point hammering it
like a stake into the ground

or planting it in a dream
or digging it up –

*

the crooked 'I'

the 'I' that's beelike, drawn to purple

the 'I' with its walk-on part

its cool green stem

From *Europa* – Bloodaxe Books Ltd

Blessing for Molly – Jo Bell

Yes, there will be times when you will have to fight.
We cannot spare you that. But then, there might
be times when you can hardly breathe for laughing.
There might be frogs in ponds to wonder at, and bumblebees
and opportunities to disappear your toes in sinking sands.
Later on, there might be days when chestnut trees are still and fat
beside a river, or the motorway. There might be beer
in paper cups, and people throwing frisbees in the park.
You might come cold and tired from work, to find
that someone's run a bath. You might see hawthorn
in an English hedgerow; catch an urban dawn
or go to bed quite drunk, with arms around you;
might feed a private hedgehog by the door one night.
There might be snowfall, bonfires, dragonflies: a hug.
And yes, there will be rain but then, there might
be rainbows. We'll be with you. You will be all right.

Coming through – Mary Anne Perkins

So this was resurrection!

A flower, pinned to the side of her hat,
gave a shout of red as if cut out for a child's
delight and ready for anything. Bold as a signal,
it helped to divert unwanted attention;

for, under the felted brim of sparrow-brown,
she was pale as a plant deprived of light too long
and aware of scrutiny: head up, eyes front;
careful not to cling on to the arm of her companion.

The pain of each step was far outdone by pleasure.
It was clear that the stream had washed each stone
for her; that the willows pressed close up to curb
the boisterous welcome of the breeze,

and every dancing leaf shone greetings back to her
in the slant of the sun. Still here, still here, it said.

From *Shadow-Play* – Indigo Dreams Publishing 2009

What the Water Gave Me (V) – Pascale Petit

after Frida Kahlo

The water enters my pores gently.
When it sings all my body listens,
the little hairs dawdle
     in calm eddies.

It is like painting then, that lost hour
when the colours play together
before becoming a mouth,
the rough face
     not yet human.

One eye drowning in its rockpool
finds a tunnel of rippled light
and opens
to gaze at its maker.
         And I,
all alone with my painted bath,
my one-thread brush
grafting skin,

my sea-changed skeleton
     a surprise reef
where fingers of live coral
knit the shattered spine.
My out-of-the-frame head
     not throbbing now.

The water a poured mirror, its song
rising up the chromatic scale
to create land on the surface.

The currents shiver like shaken glass
splashing my legs with shoals of pigment –

the blue sting, the red ache,
how art works on the pain spectrum.

From *What the Water Gave Me: Poems After Frida Kahlo* – Seren 2010

Castle Rising – Ann Phillips

To heaven with William Morris

At Castle Rising where I have never been
I sense I remember the lying of water and land
knit of the weald and pasture and high-walled orchards

There meadows are blue over green with bellflower and bugle
and banksides white over green with meadowsweet
the brook's obbligato carries the headnotes of ousels

The castle walls swim upward
its inhabitants ascendant
inside, the single harper has recovered sight
children and aged are indistinguishable
there are no clocks: hour-glasses reverse at random
and bells peal jubilee and never summons
the moss-deep carpets seem as if still untrodden
and tapestries' peacock and poppy will fade no further

At Castle Rising where I have not yet been
to fly has no need of wings
to dive no impediment of breathing
sleep is a metaphor
and wakening a continuous amazement

Deep-laid foundations bed the thrust of levitation
this is the original airship
the Bidden City

Glimmers of Hope – Anna Gibson

Hope is your open hands waiting to be filled,
Hope is the anticipation, the expectation of renewal,
The dewdrops of love that form.
I anticipate fulfilment,
The blinding intense light of happiness.
Hope is a girl that dances in the wheat field in the sun.

How bright the wit – Christopher Reid

How bright the wit,
the circumstance-mocking
theatrical badinage, burned.
To a friend concerned
she might be tired
I heard her say,
'Exhausted people
leave the hospice all day,
and I just carry on talking.'

To another, catching
a glimpse of her own
undimmable spirit:
'I'm being radiant
again, aren't I!'

It was inspired,
brave, funny and subtle
of her to interpret
the role of patient
so flat against type –
cheering her nurses,
feeding advice and support
to friends, encouraging
her husband to address his
possible future
with something of her hope.

It's not in his nature,
but he can try.

This poem is taken from *A Scattering*, Christopher Reid's tribute to his wife
Lucinda Gane, who died in October 2005. The book consists of four poetic
sequences, the first written during her final illness, the other three at intervals
after her death. *A Scattering* is published by Arete Books

Flight EZ426 – Alison Brackenbury

In Edinburgh Airport's warm afternoon
I watched a dark girl in the terminal
With eyes of shallow waters, blue and green,
Who led her small son round on a loose rein
In a calm quiet, as women walk with men.

They lean behind me now in the last lull
Before the flight; and in the throbbing plane
She speaks to his low crooning, "Look, a man."
With mustard-yellow coat, with a bleached mane,
A boy with crooked smile, a radio,
Sweeps arms with joy to tell the crew to go,
She lilts, to soothe her fright, her son, "Look, man!"

The boy sprints to a truck door, leaps inside.
Will he spring up, so young and free, again,
Shift ended, sun in eyes, his friend beside?
"We'll see Dada," she soothes. Wing tilts. Her tone
Sings to the plane's lift, "I am not alone,"
To son, to the truck cab, and on the flight,
The pilot, squinting forward into light.

*For my father and mother, who were greatly helped by a Macmillan Nurse during my
mother's final illness.*

Taking A Moment – Stephen Beattie

Snow-melt leaches from fell tops.
Windermere, as deep as longing,
mirrors March sky and ripples
with each dip of swan's beak.

Sound plays charades,
hides in sudden corners,
waits to ambush ears
with a chirring of gull wings,
or plaintive chime of hillside sheep.

A couple stands at the end of the jetty
not waiting for the ferry.
Movement is not needed to travel
on this day of possibilities.

From *Treading The Helix* – Indigo Dreams Publishing 2011

Sequence – Cathy Bryant

Love isn't fragile.
Flowers can grow through concrete.
We will beat cancer.

. She never gave in.
Laughed, joked, and always believed.
How can I do less?

Learn hope. There's such change -
the world flips in an instant,
shakes seasons and lives.

What to do when bleak?
When the flower wilts, un-blooms?
Try sowing. Growing.

At the bottom of
the pit - finding hope in the
squeeze of a friend's hand

We take you, my friend,
who thought you would be lost, gone -
take you everywhere.

Mulled Rhyme *(excerpt)* – Martin Newell

Light the coals of long-lost Christmas
Warm the place for heaven's sake
Morning frost will starch the willows
Freeze the broken-reeded lake
Dust the fields like coffee cake

Stud the orange sun with cloves
Hang it in the mulling sky
Heat the pan of days and slowly,
Let the hours liquify
Lest their flavours pass you by

Call the fleet of clouds to harbour
From the tattered sails of night
Admiral Sun to look them over
Pale Midshipman Moon in sight
Lashed to wheel in milky light

Flag the mallards down the river
Now the wild-eyed storm has gone
And the herons wait like pages
With a winter fly-past on
Heralding a whooper swan

Stifle all the whining sirens
Mute the city's drunken yells
Throng the street with laughing spirits
Light the square with carousels
Fill the air with wildheart bells

As you peer into the darkness
Listening for the midnight chime
Know there's no time like the present
Yet no present like the time
When the season's in its prime

Rooftops bathed in neon splinters
Where the shattered moonlight fell
Silence of a thousand winters
Broken by a silver bell
Merry Christmas, keep it well.

The Boat That Is My Father – Philip Gross

This is the thud
    of brass and grease
        below decks.
    This is the wheeze
of leaky valve and rusty pump,

the chug
    as it misses a beat.
        This is the mud-
clogged weary heart,
the slop to and fro in the sump,

the bilges.
    This is the spike
        on the chart, the blip
on the radar: near
now, something forming in the mist,

the scent of landfall; sometimes, fear.

Hope Hall – Hazel Buchan Cameron
for George ' Duff ' Cameron

They talk nonsense
laughed my father

Religious guff -

But I go anyway
Because it's warm
and they serve
free tea and buns.

First published in *The Currying Shop* - Imago Media 2008
Reprinted by permission of the author

Hope's Flame – Jean Harvey

When suddenly the world grows dark —
our wide horizons shrink and dim —
then Hope remains the one small spark
that glimmers, comforting within.

One candle on Life's windowsill
that offers soft its constant light
to ward off fear's approaching chill —
keeps burning through the blackest night.

Hope won't give in to gloomy thought —
resists the shadows looming where
cruel doubts creep close — Faith holds the fort
defies the clutches of despair.

Hope's flame might waver — flicker low
at times when we feel lost — alone
but through the darkness that faint glow
will surely find us — guide us home.

Woodscape – Colin Dardis

The first step in reviving a forest
Is to clear out all the dead wood
So moths can come and grace their wings
Against empty skin,

Avoiding the easy way out:
Where cycles of petrified branches
Regenerate over abandoned humus,
Blackening from neglect,

The blood and hair of woodland
Thickening into the natural pulses
Of dirt tracks and leaf-strewn mazes
Beaten cold between trees.

The autumn wind has pushed years
Through this secret little dark spot,
Exclusive to few, yet sacred
To every visited heart.

Come, let each permitted hand
Lift away an ounce of this coma,
And soon we will replevy
Our green, existent woodscape.

The C Word – U A Fanthorpe

It was a word we knew but didn't say.
I was born under the sign, but understood
People said *Crab* not *Cancer.*

Routinely he grew a beard every winter
For his annual bronchitis. *Dad's cough whiskers*
We called it, being young and excitable,
Thrilled by changes in the parental landscape.
In the spring he'd get better.

In the spring, when I was older,
Free to roam London, I collected his order
From the shop in Piccadilly: *State Express Three Fives.*
They were dear. *Coffin nails*, we called them.,
Being young and flighty.

We took the ten-foot dinghy up the dark river.
He was heavy, unmechanical. The temperamental outboard
Stalled at Henley; we grappled with it,
Ran out of money, had a lot of grubby fun.
Everyone called him *Sir.*

He loved water, and words. On his deathbed
He tested me on how to pronounce
Humour and *indissoluble.* Of course he was right.

Near the end, he lost part of a tooth. He'd always
Looked spry before. The broken-ness haunted me.
I hoped he didn't know.

What did he know? Mother told us not to say.
He doesn't know. It's better for him not to.

I thought he knew. A look in his eye.
But being gentle, preferred to spare us knowledge.
We pretended innocence, pretended he'd recover.

He was a judge. He understood *sentencing.*
On his way up the dark river, he chose
Silence as companion, among all those words.
I wish we could have spoken, shared his knowledge.
In the spring he died.

From *New and Collected Poems* (2010) - Enitharmon Press. (Permission acknowledgement R V Bailey).

Metaphysical – Carole Baldock

They say if there were a mountain 1000 miles high
and once in every 1000 years, a little bird came by
to sharpen its beak, til there was no mountain left at last
only one moment in Time is all that has passed.

Then how is it that I was born just the other day
yet 60 years have come and gone, as if I'd slept it all away?
So if I caught that little bird, its outlook would be rough -
because I'd wring its bloody neck and have the bugger stuffed.

Published in *Bitching* - Sound Publications

Still – Anna Dickie

Symmetrical
in our imperfection -
the exposed ribs,
the join-up-the-dot tattoos
forever inking in what's missing.
Two friends, two breasts,
two crosses, two cards marked,
scratched, sniffed. Two almost
lucky winners. Stirred and shaken
into this, the glorious holding pattern
that we photographed today.

Look, it says
                still life -
still love.

This poem was first published in my pamphlet Heart Notes,
ISBN: 978-1-902629-13-1, which was written after my treatment and published
by Colin Will at Calder Wood Press.

The Trees in All their Wisdom – Liz Loxley

How we decipher the wind in their lurch
and lift; their quality of knuckling down;
the cutlery of their branches, as forks
clack in compartments of sky; how they brush
birds into being with two eyebrowed strokes;
how they feather their fingers, giving high
fives; the way they balance the whole wide sky
on the flat of their palms; how they invoke
spirits of the woodland with windchime chants;
how they hollow themselves to keep secrets
that tick in the dark like black-backed beetles;
how they roll with thunder, the belly laugh
of their storm-split trunks; their V sign to death;
the star-spinning span of them; ocean-depth.

Rain song – John Siddique

On the third day of the British rainy season,
in a café fogged by breath, coffee steam, moisture
from fried breakfasts. The relief of getting
them off to school, the quick stop before knuckling
down to the day. The rain turns on,
words like bucketing and pouring,
words like downpour and monsoon.

The sound comes up, and everyone stops,
stops eating, stops talking, all eyes turn
to the grey fogged window, all eyes begin
slow smiles. We nestle into the rain-song
as if it were a duvet and we're hiding
upstairs, a game with our mum and dad.
No one will be the first to speak,
to give the game away.

From *Full Blood* - Salt 2011

Wedding Song – Bob Dylan

I love you more than ever, more than time and more than love
I love you more than money and more than the stars above
Love you more than madness, more than waves upon the sea
Love you more than life itself, you mean that much to me

Ever since you walked right in, the circle's been complete
I've said goodbye to haunted rooms and faces in the street
To the courtyard of the jester which is hidden from the sun
I love you more than ever and I haven't yet begun

You breathed on me and made my life a richer one to live
When I was deep in poverty you taught me how to give
Dried the tears up from my dreams and pulled me from the hole
Quenched my thirst and satisfied the burning in my soul

You gave me babies one, two, three, what is more, you saved my life
Eye for eye and tooth for tooth, your love cuts like a knife
My thoughts of you don't ever rest, they'd kill me if I lie
I'd sacrifice the world for you and watch my senses die

The tune that is yours and mine to play upon this earth
We'll play it out the best we know, whatever it is worth
What's lost is lost, we can't regain what went down in the flood
But happiness to me is you and I love you more than blood

It's never been my duty to remake the world at large
Nor is it my intention to sound a battle charge
'Cause I love you more than all of that with a love that doesn't bend
And if there is eternity I'd love you there again

Oh, can't you see that you were born to stand by my side
And I was born to be with you, you were born to be my bride
You're the other half of what I am, you're the missing piece
And I love you more than ever with that love that doesn't cease

You turn the tide on me each day and teach my eyes to see
Just bein' next to you is a natural thing for me
And I could never let you go, no matter what goes on
'Cause I love you more than ever now that the past is gone

A Good Morning – Charlie Jordan

Still half asleep, I watch you at the sink.
Broad shoulders tanned, old Levi's hug your waist.
You're 'Marlon Brando beautiful' I think,
the mirror shows that lethal smile in place.
Hot flannel first, to wake up every pore;
this morning ritual so masculine.
Then badger brush whirls foam from soap before
it glides along the contours of your chin.
You reach down for a blade then pause to see
me gazing at each muscle that you flex.
The razor slaloms stubble lazily;
you rinse, towel dry and tease me that I'm next.
I love watching you shave, you artisan…
defining what it is to be a man.

Possibilities – Gill Learner

All through her teens she dreamed – of hitch-hiking
to Paris where she'd yawn onto a hose-wet square
or south to an aching back between strips of vines.

She could have minded kids in a kibbutz; become
a Ten Pound Pom – learned to shoot rabbits, swim
with one eye skinned for sharks. But it was never time.

Transferred to City branch, she hunkered in a Morris van
down the M1, shared a hostel room with Jean
from Deal, kissed several men, married an optician

with a dread of planes so they honeymooned in Poole;
progressed to yearly sandcastles at Ilfracombe; later
struck out for Wimereux, then Brittany and Dordogne.

Atlas to hand, by text and web she follows children,
grandchildren, to Prague, Algiers, Ontario; frets about
dysentery in Kathmandu, giardia in Kuantan and

as Saturdays creak past explores the travel section first,
shrugs off his frowns. There's a gathering
between her shoulder blades – she's making plans.

Family Tree – Michael Schmidt

Watching his creatures with a filial sorrow
Christ, not a shepherd yet, not yet a man,
Propped on a cloud at the edge of things, his hands,
Unbroken, on his hips, wonders who he'll be
And knows it's up to Adam to determine
What human pleasure might feel like, and what pain,
To the Son of God -- Adam who's in mourning,
Adam whose Maker has withdrawn the Kingdom
All for a fruit, a serpent and a rib.
The Son of God sees Eve grow plump as a pillow
Bearing a mallet and three nails inside her,
Bearing a spear, a sponge and vinegar.

Journey – Roselle Angwin

The land streams past the window.
The heart asks for both clarity and paradox,
aches equally for freedom and for joining,
being part of and apart.

Oh to be like a tree. To be that horse
dreaming, one hoof delicately pointed,
muzzle lowered and relaxed,
at home completely in the day.

Tell me the truest thing you can,
is what this journey seems to say.

From *All the missing names of love* – Indigo Dreams Publishing 2011

Miracle – Seamus Heaney

Not the one who walks away
But the ones who have known him all along
And carry him in —

Their shoulders numb, the ache and stoop deeplocked
In their backs, the stretcher handles
Slippery with sweat. And no let up

Until he's strapped on tight, made tiltable
And raised to the hot tiles, then lowered for healing.
Be mindful of them as they stand and wait

For the burn of the paid-out ropes to cool,
Their slight light-headedness and incredulity
To pass, those ones who had known him all along.

By kind permission of the author, from *Human Chain* - Faber & Faber, 2010

The Opportune Moment – Sheenagh Pugh

"If you were waiting for the opportune moment, that was it" –
Capt. Jack Sparrow, Pirates of the Caribbean; Curse of the Black Pearl

When you go ashore in that town,
take neither a camera nor a notebook.
However many photographs you upload
of that street, the smell of almond paste
will be missing; the harbour will not sound
of wind slapping on chains. You will read
notes like "Sami church", later, and know
you saw nothing, never put it where
you could find it again, were never
really there. When you go ashore
in the small port with the rusty trawlers,
there will be fur hawkers who all look
like Genghis Khan on a market stall,
crumbling pavements, roses frozen in bud,
an altar with wool hangings, vessels
like canal ware, a Madonna
with a Russian doll face. When you go
ashore, take nothing but the knowledge
that where you are, you never will be again.

From *Long-Haul Travellers* - Seren

Jervis Pearson Ward, Nottingham City Hospital, February 2009 – Drew Wilkie

I have walked amongst giants hewn from solid oak and granite
Reduced to splinters and sand
And women so ravaged that all that is left is their beauty from within.

We are the cancer community – a brotherhood so strong
That we will kick the arse of this vile disease
And god help anyone who gets in our way!

We may be dribbling, incontinent, sometimes vague
But we are on a mission that only we truly understand
So please remember that when we appear to take no prisoners!

Dear Jo – Irma Upex-Huggins

In faith and prayers you went with me
into the raging fears and frozen grief
I was cut from all sense of who I am

when thoughts inhabited worlds
when days had neither sun nor moon
when collusion in my belly held secrets
when the out-of-sight bleeding was safe
when I crossed the mountain unseeing

I walked vexed in nights
that brought not sleep but
cathedrals of lullabies from the abyss
shapeless shadows on wings seducing
moods like bad wind abandoning me
to the decay of dark unknowable fear
to the vicissitudes of a body colonised

You did not cower from shouts at devils
nor chide my rejection of angels
You held for me the paradox
and reached deep into the chaos
to where I could forgive the moon
and the sun for the violence.

Seasons Pass – Kate Edwards

Midsummer nights,
jasmine, honeysuckle
hanging from walls,
clematis clinging purple
against a hedge of roses,
shades paling in dusk,
dreams of a summer past
hanging on the air.

Dreams of another garden
where you kissed me,
your lips hard on mine
taking my soft breath;
night of strange magic.

Then winter comes,
icicles hang from walls,
stark black the trees
against a charcoal sky,
the flowers withered,
love turned to frost,
a passing seasonal love
that faded with the cold.

Spring will awaken,
aroma of blossom
exhaling into the air,
daffodils crowd the borders,
leaves unfurl in relief,
Spring returning, and so will you.

The Toast – Jean L. Kreiling

He leaned back in his chair and said, "Now *this*
is living!"—his familiar exclamation,
made every evening, not with artifice
or irony, but as a declaration
of simple truth. Perhaps it was a warning
that joy depends on recognizing it,
that every time we see another morning
we've won big without realizing it.
He said it mostly to himself, however,
not really preaching to us, and he raised
a glass of wine, or gin, or juice, but never
drank much; the toast itself sufficed. He praised
existence—nothing more, and nothing less:
he had the gift of grateful consciousness

The Path – Norman Buller

I sing of the immortal journey
of creation scattered over the world,
of rain sent from the drenching sky
to quicken the dead earth.

You are a raindrop in the ocean,
a grain of sand on the beach of the world,
a spec of dust in the shifting wind;
walk in humility.

I sing of created male and female,
union of lover and beloved.
Plant your tree and nurture it
in the orchard of Truth.

Cross the bridge sharper than a sword
and thinner than a single hair;
follow the caravan of Love
wherever its camels turn.

On Roses – Clare Crossman

Old fashioned to say I would like
to praise roses: the way the petals
keep their scent, and colour stays
in the last threads long after they have fallen.

Also, the way they ask for names:
Margaret Merrill, Duchess, Honesty,
and leap, to garlands and headdresses,
adorning buttonholes and hair.
Or bunched for anniversaries, proposals,
they make it easy to embrace,
and believe that time will wait.

There are the stories they attract:
symbol of two counties each with
a perfect heart, or the power it was
thought they had to comfort the mad.
How when they are thrown into a grave
they will remain until their velvet dissolves
to water. But then their scent in June
returns warmth, newness, the damask of a shawl.

Outside my house dog roses arch and climb,
wild on the fences, heedless among
the hedges. Going back to somewhere
at which I can only guess,
or believe that I remember.

Recovering – Jane Weir

When I cough no matter whether
it's short and raspy or endless
like a marching army on slush and ice,
you're attentive. You always get up,
answer with a look, always follow
up with deft touches.
Half awake I watch you light
our bedroom fire — the room's
Moscow in winter.
You pull up a stick chair, open
your serious book. I silhouette
the side of your face with my eyes
and think of Tolstoy,
your other family, our child
who's due in a month.
Now that I'm slowly getting better
you surprise me, etch my name
in ice on the window pane,
investing in a still from my favourite film.
Today you bring a wad
of sunflowers into the room.
I am full of sleep,
secretly you had positioned them
so that when I wake
I can observe them
from our bed, their petals tigering
through an alchemy of winter light.
If spies had pressed their faces
to the glass they would have seen us.
We were the two figures skating.

From *The Way I Dressed During The Revolution* - Templar Poetry

The Bird Cure – Chris McCabe

I was poking tarmac for mauve Twenties when the kingfisher cashed
    its azure bullion.
It had been a long night of slow .wav downloads, then you showed me
    a dawn of the redwings.
I couldn't find an oak to guarantee my chequebook but you had a wren
    as pocketchange.
Oil had slicked my best black shoes but a starling flashed green
    its Pacific dorsal.
My wardrobe was for so long monotone but the goldfinch always wore
    the same red ruff.
I thought nothing varied more than my moods but the lakeside
    understood so many warblers.
Palpitations artexed a brush-in-the-eye but the woodpecker's pointillism
    was precise.
A heart-in-the-mouth boiled a sunny-side breakfast but the robin was
    a cardiac in an eggcup.
The train through the country had its own dawn plumage but the owl
    was a disgraced Quaker.
I thought it was just me that wore a nightsky on my back but the black-
    bird sheened to olive-green.
The agent pitched a bachelor pad of luxury but the docks exchanged
    the bullfinches' shrapnel.
The pain paused its industrial-estate massage while the gulls carouselled
    so many playgrounds.
Thoughts were muscle-sprung-to-wing but the peewit whirred itself
    to danger - that's what you do -
    take the mess away out of love.
The GP issued SSRIs on the nightshift but each morning's call brought
    the bird cure.

A-Shelling Peas – Harry Breaker Morant

Now, all the world is green and bright
Outside the latticed pane;
The fields are decked with gold and white,
And Spring has come again.
But though the world be fair without,
With flow'rs and waving trees,
'Tis pleasanter to be about
Where Nell's a-shelling peas.

Her eyes are blue as cloudless skies,
And dimples deck her cheeks;
Whilst soft lights loiter in her eyes
Whene'er she smiles or speaks.
So all the sunlit morning-tide
I dally at mine ease,
To loaf at slender Nelly's side
When Nell's a-shelling peas.

This bard, who sits a-watching Nell,
With fingers white and slim,
Owns up that, as she breaks each shell,
She also "breaks up" him;
And could devoutly drop upon
Submissive, bended knees
To worship Nell with apron on -
A saint a-shelling peas.

The tucked-up muslin sleeves disclose
Her round arms white and bare -
'Tis only "shelling peas" that shows
Those dainty dimples there.
Old earth owns many sights to see
That captivate and please; -
The most bewitching sight for me
Is Nell a-shelling peas.

Still I Rise – Maya Angelou

You may write me down in history
With your bitter, twisted lies,
You may trod me in the very dirt
But still, like dust, I'll rise.

Does my sassiness upset you?
Why are you beset with gloom?
'Cause I walk like I've got oil wells
Pumping in my living room.

Just like moons and like suns,
With the certainty of tides,
Just like hopes springing high,
Still I'll rise.

Did you want to see me broken?
Bowed head and lowered eyes?
Shoulders falling down like teardrops,
Weakened by my soulful cries.

Does my haughtiness offend you?
Don't you take it awful hard
'Cause I laugh like I got gold mines
Diggin' in my own back yard.

You may shoot me with your words,
You may cut me with your eyes,
You may kill me with your hatefulness,
But still, like air, I'll rise.

Does my sexiness upset you?
Does it come as a surprise
That I dance like I've got diamonds
At the meeting of my thighs?

Out of the huts of history's shame
I rise
Up from a past that's rooted in pain
I rise
I'm a black ocean, leaping and wide,
Welling and swelling I bear in the tide.

Leaving behind nights of terror and fear
I rise
Into a daybreak that's wondrously clear
I rise
Bringing the gifts my ancestors gave,
I am the dream and the hope of the slave.
I rise
I rise
I rise.

INDEX

275

Indigo Dreams Publishing
132 Hinckley Road
Stoney Stanton
Leicestershire
LE9 4LN
UK
www.indigodreams.co.uk